TIME MANAGEMENT
FOR THE
CREATIVE PERSON

• • • • •

OTHER BOOKS BY LEE SILBER

Aim First!

Successful San Diegans

Notes, Quotes & Advice

Dating in San Diego

TIME
MANAGEMENT
FOR THE
Creative
PERSON

. . . . .

Lee Silber

THREE RIVERS PRESS   NEW YORK

Post-it™ is a registered trademark of 3M
Mind Mapping™ is a registered trademark of Tony Buzan

Published by Three Rivers Press, 201 East 50th Street, New York,
New York 10022. Member of the Crown Publishing Group.

Random House, Inc. New York, Toronto, London, Sydney,
Auckland
www.randomhouse.com

THREE RIVERS PRESS and colophon are trademarks of Crown
Publishers, Inc.

Printed in the United States of America

Design by June Bennett-Tantillo

Library of Congress Cataloging-in-Publication Data
Silber, Lee T.
    Time management for the creative person / Lee Silber — 1st ed.
        p.   cm.
    Includes bibliographical references and index.
    1. Time management.   I. Title.
HD69.T54S575   1998
640'.43—dc21   97-37298
                                                         CIP

ISBN 0-609-80090-6

10 9 8 7 6 5 4 3

To all those creative people who have been
ridiculed, reprimanded, and rejected
because of their slightly unorthodox
right-brain way of doing things.
It's payback time.

Contents

• • • • •

Acknowledgments

• • • • •

Behind the author of nearly every book stand several people, whose names when mentioned are deservedly preceded with the words "without whom this book would not be possible." Boy, is that ever true in my case—starting with . . .

My agent, Toni Lopopolo, without whom I wouldn't have had the opportunity to write this book. Thank you for your belief in me from proposal to publication.

My editors (as an author you consider yourself extremely fortunate to have a good one—I had two great ones!) Peter Ginna, who got the ball rolling before moving on to Oxford Press, and Patrick Sheehan, who took the ball and ran with it (scoring a game-winning touchdown in the process).

My writing partner, Beth Hagman, who has been dotting my *t*'s and crossing my *i*'s (see why she's so important?) since my second of six books. This is one "without whom" I hope to continue to count on for years to come. Thank you, Beth!

My good friend and colleague Harriet Schechter, who recommended me for this project. Your vote of confidence was the start of a cycle of events that has changed my life. It is impossible to measure a mentor's impact on a mentee, so it is safe to say Harriet has helped me immeasurably.

My wife, whose support while I was writing this book included screening my calls and wisely telling visitors, "He's not well, he's writing a book." Thank you for making sure I came through this well nourished and reasonably sane (and loved).

My heartfelt thanks to all the authors, artists, actors, entrepreneurs, and experts who agreed to share their insights and ideas to help make this a better book. Your willingness to help others (and me) should most certainly earn you much good karma on all your future projects.

My "without whom" citations would not be complete if

I didn't acknowledge the many authors and their books who came before mine, laying a foundation with their ground-breaking work that this book is built on: Julia Cameron, Ann McGee Cooper, Sunny Schlenger, Stephanie Winston, Jeffrey Mayer, Marilee Zdenek, Eric Maisel, SARK, Joyce Wycoff, Dorothy Lehmkuhl, and Dolores Cotter Lamping. There are far too many to mention them all here (see bibliography), but you know who you are. You are to be commended.

Finally, to the hundreds of creative people who, during the course of the past two years, willingly agreed to share their most intimate time and organizational challenges with me in hopes that I would come up with workable solutions (I kept my promise)—this book is for you.

Preface

· · · · · ·

HOW TO GET THE MOST FROM THIS BOOK

*Advice is what we ask for when we already know the
answer but wish we didn't.*

—Erica Jong

There is no right or wrong way to read this book—just read
it. Knowing your tendency to jump around, I made each
chapter stand alone so you can jump in wherever you like.
Test the water first, then dive in and read the rest. There are
enough fresh ideas in here to organize an army of artists. It's
a grab bag of user-friendly tips—so many, in fact, that I guarantee you will discover something you can use to help manage your time more effectively no matter how chaotic your
life is now.

This is a real how-to, solution-oriented book, so it is
important that you use and abuse it. Mix and match the ideas
presented to find solutions to fit your unique personality, situation, and needs. Experiment, explore—do what comes naturally. There are no absolutes here. In fact, many of the
suggestions are antithetical to each other and to accepted time
management rules. Most are easy to implement (you can use
them right out of the box) and incorporate into your lifestyle
without going through culture shock or a personality change.

Circle, highlight, or make a note next to the suggestions
that sound as though they will work for you—and please, try
them on for size before discarding them. Start out with a
small thing, a simple thing—but take on only one thing at a
time. Don't overwhelm yourself. Give yourself a chance to
make it work.

As I was writing this book, I hung a sign on the wall
above my desk to remind me that in order for you to embrace

time management, it must be "fast, flexible, fun, and functional." I tried to stick to the "keep it simple, make it fun" approach throughout, so you wouldn't feel threatened or get bored. Judge for yourself, but I believe you will find at least some of my ideas fit right in with your natural way of doing things. The goal is to create positive and lasting change that will improve your life for years to come.

Finally, you will notice that this book is filled with an abundance of stories, anecdotes, interviews, quotes, metaphors, and a whole lot of humor. These examples back up the points and make the book an easy read. This is serious stuff, sure, but we can have a little fun at the same time. Right?

WHY I WROTE THE BOOK

Life is five percent joy, five percent grief, and ninety percent maintenance. Make the maintenance more efficient and enjoyable and you are increasing your joy quotient by a lot.

—Harriet Schechter

There is a saying that goes, "I see feathers on it, but it's still not flying. Let's toss it around and see if it makes salad." That's how I feel about 99 percent of the other books written on time management. They rehash a lot of the same old stuff, presented to you with a new title and cover—a one-size-fits-all approach that just doesn't work for many people.

Do we need another book on time management? I believe we do—a completely different one. That's what I set out to do, a simple, solution-oriented book with ideas that really work—in the real world, for real people with real problems.

How do I know they will work? First of all, I am not an armchair quarterback. I'm just like you, a creative person afflicted with some of the same time-related dilemmas that seem to rob us of more and more of our time. As an artist, author, musician, entrepreneur, lecturer, and on-air personality, I am always looking for ways to get more things done (and still have fun). So I personally took a test drive with these ideas before trying to sell them to you. I kicked the tires and road-tested them and included only the best, the ones that really worked well for me or someone I know, under all kinds of conditions.

I put my heart and soul into making this the best book it could be. I hope it shows.

IF YOU READ THIS BOOK

Counting time is not so important as making time count.

—*James Walker*

I'm operating on the assumption here that you want to change, that you feel you have a problem handling your time and keeping your life organized. That's why you bought this book. So don't feel I'm criticizing when I suggest tactics to improve your life.

Like it or not, you'll learn some things about yourself here. You'll ask yourself some hard questions—and the answers will set you free.

There are several concepts central to effective time management that you can make work for you—and none of them start with cleaning off your desk. I don't think the changes you need to make are big or many. But the effect on your life and your happiness can be huge.

Picture yourself driving through a thick fog. Your hands, the knuckles white, grip the wheel as you try to anticipate what dangers lie ahead. You hope for the best and anticipate the worst. The situation is totally out of your control. What if I told you that if you hang in there, eventually the sky will turn blue and you can get back up to speed, put the top down, and let the wind rush through your hair as you drive down the road of life—in control, enjoying the ride with a clear vision of what's ahead. That's what this book can do for you.

What this book *won't* do, however, is help you win the Good Housekeeping Seal of Approval. It won't even attempt to turn you into a compulsive timesaving freak trying to squeeze one more worthless task into your day. Puleeeze. This book is about working with your strengths, about learning a new habit or two, about doing some minor tweaking to free up small chunks of time (which eventually add up to hours saved) for lasting and positive change. To control the chaos, yes, but not so much so that it stifles your creativity.

Life is not orderly (or perfect). It is rich and fascinating and exciting, and meant to be lived to its fullest. Use this book to help you live that life, and you will make me very proud.

TIME MANAGEMENT
FOR THE
CREATIVE PERSON

• • • • •

1
•••••
I THINK YOU'RE GREAT!

Truths and Half-Truths about the Creative Person

We change our opinions of ourselves so often. What the outside world thinks is only a small part of the image.

—*Carly Simon*

Jim Leyritz, a catcher for the California Angels, found that pitchers were having a hard time seeing his signals during night games. (A catcher will hold down fingers between his legs to indicate what he wants the pitcher to throw—fastball, curveball, slider, and so on.) His solution? Use correction fluid to paint his fingers white. That's one very creative ball player.

By the way, did you know that correction fluid's inventor, Betty Nesmith, was an executive secretary in 1951 when she concocted a white liquid that bonded with paper to conceal typing errors? She sold her company in 1974 for nearly $50 million!

The point is painters, writers, and musicians don't have a monopoly on creativity. Creativity isn't a function of the job you do—ever hear of creative accounting?—it has to do with the way you see things. It's a multilevel approach to life and work and everything in it.

Even janitors can be creative. The El Cortez Hotel was the first skyscraper built in San Diego. After some years of operation, the management realized they needed a second elevator. A janitor overheard the architects and engineers discussing the best way to cut a hole in the lobby floor to accommodate another shaft and came up with a solution that would allow the hotel to stay open during construction (and save his job). As he leaned on his mop, he suggested casually, "Why not build the elevator on the *outside* of the hotel?" This idea was unheard of at the time, but it worked.

You are born with the natural ability to be creative, but you don't necessarily keep it. Research shows that 90 percent of five-year-olds are creative, but only 2 percent of adults are. What happens? The scientific explanation is that you learn to rely more on the left side of your brain (the rational side). The simple explanation is that the muse gets flabby from lack of use. Either use it or lose it.

A rich, vivid imagination and that anything-is-possible attitude are suppressed or stifled early on by parents and teachers ("Draw inside the lines") and later by bosses and corporations ("We've always done it this way"). Worse still, you do it to yourself, saying things like "I can't draw" or "I can't spell."

Creative careers often involve some element of risk, and well-meaning parents and peers might discourage you from taking a chance. But some people slip through the cracks, keeping that creative spark alive no matter what. There are also those who were creative as kids but are unable to find an outlet for their creativity as adults, and even a few who learn how to take advantage of their right-brain assets much later in life.

This book is for the closet creative as well as the career creative—and it's surprising how many people fit into those two categories.

ABOUT THE CREATIVE PERSONALITY

Every creative person is a duality or a synthesis of contradictory aptitudes.

—Carl Jung

Creatives are special, unique, wonderful people, no doubt about it. Maybe you feel a little out of step with the rest of the world. It's not easy being a creative person. Being an original—or even a little bit different—opens you up to ridicule and persecution.

In the movie *Powder*, a bald, albino teenager is found living in the basement of his parents' home. A social worker tries to bring him into mainstream society, which rejects his genius and unique powers. A similar theme runs through the movie *Phenomenon*, starring John Travolta. People are afraid of what they don't understand and fight to suppress originality and creativity at every step.

R. Buckminster Fuller (inventor, architect, scientist, engineer, author) is responsible for the invention, development, and implementation of some great ideas. He holds 170 patents and has authored 24 books. Yet he was expelled from Harvard and labeled a "kook" because his ideas were so outrageous. It didn't matter that his ideas worked—they were simply head of their time.

Steve Jobs's father, tired of his tinkering in the garage, told him to make something salable or get a job. A few months later the first Apple computer was sold. There are hundreds of stories like this, and each one points out that we, as a society, as a world, desperately need creatives. They fuel our progress.

"Don't compromise yourself. You are all you got," said Janis Joplin.

If you make it to adulthood with that creative spark intact, it's likely to keep you going forever. It's like breathing. Sam Spears, an inventor of toys with Hasbro (responsible for Lite-Brite, Mr. Potato Head, and G.I. Joe), retired years ago but still continues to invent at the age of seventy.

MYTHS ABOUT THE CREATIVE PERSON

The creative person is the master rather than the slave of his imagination.

—Michael LeBoeuf, Ph.D.

"The great myth (and barrier) for creative people is the belief that their creativity precludes them from being organized. The reality is that their disorganization can get in the way of their creativity," says organizer Odette Pollar.

I agree. The answer is to use your strengths and get organized in creative ways.

First, however, you're going to have to get over some silly ideas you might have about yourself and the way you work.

YOU HAVE UNLIMITED ENERGY. *Nobody* has unlimited energy. You may be special, but you're still human. You need to focus what energy you have on things you are passionate about. And you need some level of time management and organization to keep you from getting distracted and wasting yourself on the small stuff.

YOU'RE LAZY. Actually, a creative is always working. "It takes a heap of loafing to write a book," says Gertrude Stein. If you *look* lazy, it's because you're not working on what someone else wants you to work on, or the way they want you to work. Or it could be you are blocked—by fear, for one thing. Paralyzed by too many choices, by perfectionism, by lack of resources. Organization can keep this from happening, or at least keep it under control.

YOU LACK FOLLOW-THROUGH. Easily distracted, yes. "Helped are those who create anything at all, for they shall relive the thrill of their own conception," says Alice Walker. But sometimes follow-through simply means handing off the job to someone who can do the finish work better, faster, cheaper.

YOU'RE IRRESPONSIBLE. People are likely to see you this way when you're constantly late, forget meetings, don't return calls, ignore friends, miss deadlines, don't do your share around the house, and so forth. It could just be that your priorities are different. Learning how to set priorities can help you get past this stumbling block—but don't expect that your priorities will ever be the same as everybody else's.

YOU HATE STRUCTURE. Actually, you need *some* structure in your life to allow your creativity free rein. Chaos is not creative. But there are all kinds of structures. If you don't find one you like, build your own.

YOU'RE IMPULSIVE. Well, okay, this one probably isn't a myth. But you can learn to stop and think—yes, you can.

PROBLEMS WE ALL FACE

Commandment number one of any truly civilized society is this: Let people be different.
—David Grayson

In the movie *Twister* you get the sense of the awesome power of a tornado. It randomly picks things up and hurls them about as it swirls out of control, leaving a swath of destruction. Ever feel your life is like that?

There are forces at work that you simply can't control, and no matter how fast you run you can't get ahead of them. They just keep gaining on you, wreaking havoc on your time, your life. You can't run, you can't hide (as much as you would like to crawl into the cellar and bolt the door). The pace of modern life is insane. Things change so fast, we can hardly keep up. Or have they really changed that much? Read the following editorial:

> Try as you will, you get behind in the race, in spite of yourself. It's an incessant strain to keep pace. . . . And still you lose ground. Science empties its discoveries on you so fast that you stagger beneath them in

hopeless bewilderment. . . . Everything is high pressure. Human nature can't endure much more.

It was run in the *Atlantic Journal* on June 16, 1833. (That's right, 1833!) Different century, same problems. The radio commentator Paul Harvey said, "In times like these, it helps to recall that there have always been times like these."

Still, I have to admit, time management problems today are far more complex than they were a hundred years ago. Consider:

- Everyone's busy; even "retired" people have full schedules. The average lifespan is twice what it was a hundred years ago, yet you're very aware of how short life is. You want to spend it as well as you can.

- People are overwhelmed and frazzled by the complexity, pace, quantity of information, and number of choices we face. Should I have decaf or regular? A latte, espresso, or mocha? Sugar? Who knows—I have too much on my mind to decide.

- People are working longer hours (this is a simple fact), but there is no increase in disposable income and certainly no lessening of personal responsibility. In fact, many baby boomers are facing the prospect of caring for their elderly parents while still caring for their own homes and families.

- Americans aren't getting enough sleep, but it is socially unacceptable in this country to take a catnap to catch up.

- It's getting harder to keep up with everyday chores, even with every modern tool and convenience. The lawn looks like tundra, the kids are wearing their socks inside out (until you can get to the laundry), and you keep saying you're going to get to the gym (you keep paying the dues). There just isn't enough time.

- Technology that was supposed to save us, make life easier, has become a burden in itself. You have to learn how to use it, relearn it when something new comes along, and sometimes teach it to others. By the time you get the hang of it, it's obsolete.

- By trying to cram as much as they can into their day, many people are missing out on life. Worse, you think this is what you *should* be doing. So you have no time to stop, to think, to find a better way.

LEFT-BRAIN, RIGHT-BRAIN (NO-BRAINER QUIZ)

We use both hemispheres of our brains at different times in different situations, though many people favor one hemisphere over the other. This is a test (and only a test) to determine which "style" you prefer and what hemisphere of the brain dominates your thinking.

Relax, there is no pass or fail, and there are no wrong answers. Just choose the answer that comes closest to describing you.

1. When meeting someone
   a. I usually show up early or on time.
   b. I am usually running a teensy-weensie bit late.

2. Sticking to plans makes me
   a. feel safe and secure.
   b. feel as if I'm locked in a very small closet.

3. When someone interrupts me, I find it
   a. annoying.
   b. stimulating.

4. At the beginning of the workday
   a. I make a list of things to do and plan my day around my list.
   b. I shuffle through the piles of papers on my desk before I finally decide what to do first.

5. Daydreaming is
   a. a waste of time.
   b. the best part of my day.

6. When faced with a decision,

    a. I weigh all my options and make a decision based on the facts at hand.

    b. I go with my instincts.

7. When learning how to use a new piece of equipment,

    a. I read the instruction manual before beginning.

    b. I jump in and wing it. (If all else fails, I'll look at the manual.)

8. When it comes to time,

    a. I have a good sense of time but frequently look at my watch just to double-check.

    b. I never know what time it is, and I usually don't wear a watch.

9. When someone gives me directions, I prefer to

    a. have them written out (with street names).

    b. have them draw me a map with landmarks and visual references.

10. At this minute, my checking account is

    a. balanced to the penny.

    b. overdrawn (I think). I do not keep a running balance.

11. When I'm shopping and I see something I want to buy,

    a. I save up until I have the money.

    b. I charge it (You only live once, baby).

12. When faced with a stupid rule or instructions,

    a. I follow instructions but complain.

    b. I bend the rules and take the consequences.

13. When I am telling a story to a friend,

    a. I will cut to the chase (I use the phrase "yada, yada, yada" a great deal).

    b. I am very animated and likely to get sidetracked.

14. I feel that risk taking is

    a. well, risky. (To be avoided whenever possible.)

    b. part of life. Go for it!

15. When it comes to doing my taxes,
- **a.** I have all my receipts in order before I start and read IRS code in my free time.
- **b.** I take my shoebox of receipts and dump it on my accountant's desk.

16. When it comes to my personality,
- **a.** I am loyal and dependable.
- **b.** I have been called a jokester and prankster. I am known for my sense of humor.

17. On weekends, I
- **a.** make a "things to do" list.
- **b.** do whatever I feel like doing, whenever I feel like doing it. I may do nothing.

18. On vacation
- **a.** I have already read books on the destination and made an itinerary.
- **b.** I wing it. I'm on vacation, aren't I?

19. When I cook,
- **a.** I find a good recipe and follow it carefully.
- **b.** I find an interesting recipe and add a little of this, substitute a little of that. I never cook anything the same way twice.

20. When it comes to making decisions,
- **a.** I usually decide right away and stick to it.
- **b.** I postpone making a choice and change my mind often.

21. When faced with an unpleasant task,
- **a.** I prefer to do it a little at a time, step by step.
- **b.** I either jump in and do it all at once or put it off and hope it goes away.

22. When I have been faced with major changes in my life, I found it
- **a.** terrifying.
- **b.** exciting.

23. If Martha Stewart came to my house,
 - **a.** she'd comment on the cleanliness and suggest some crafts projects.
 - **b.** she'd run screaming back out into the street.

24. My work space looks like
 - **a.** the top of an aircraft carrier (nothing lying around).
 - **b.** Disneyland (neat stuff and office toys at every turn).

25. When it comes to paper,
 - **a.** I like to file it.
 - **b.** I like to pile it.

26. When it comes to implementing a project, I am likely to be asked to
 - **a.** handle the step-by-step planning and implementation.
 - **b.** come up with ideas and deal with the big picture.

27. When it comes to finding things,
 - **a.** there is a place for everything and everything is in its place.
 - **b.** I am constantly looking for keys, phone numbers, and so on.

28. When it comes to remembering things I have to do,
 - **a.** I remember every little detail.
 - **b.** What was the question again?

29. When it comes to long-range planning,
 - **a.** I know what I will be doing for New Year's Eve 2015.
 - **b.** I like to keep my options open.

30. People describe me as
 - **a.** level-headed (unemotional).
 - **b.** a roller coaster of emotions (passionate).

31. In a nutshell, my work style is like this:
 - **a.** I tend to concentrate on one task at a time; I'm easily overwhelmed.
 - **b.** I like to juggle several things at once.

32. For touchy matters, I prefer to
 - **a.** write a memo.
 - **b.** meet face-to-face.

33. When reading a magazine,
  a. I start at page one and read in a sequential order.
  b. I jump in wherever looks most interesting.

34. When asked a question,
  a. I figure there is either a right or wrong answer (things are black and white).
  b. I try to figure out where the question is coming from.

35. When asked for my opinion, I
  a. think before I speak.
  b. say what's on my mind (foot-in-mouth syndrome).

36. When it comes to projects,
  a. I am known for my stick-to-itiveness.
  b. I know to start things and I always intend to finish them, but . . .

Total number of "A" answers: _22_
Total number of "B" answers: ____

If you have twenty-five or more "A" answers, you can consider yourself left-brain dominant. Give this book to your partner.

If you have twenty-five or more "B" answers, you're a right-brainer (Hooray!).

Otherwise you can consider yourself whole brained or at least partly lateralized. (Bravo!)

LEFT BRAIN/RIGHT BRAIN

Break on through to the other side.

—Jim Morrison

Everyone is wired differently, but there are patterns of behavior that most of us follow. Oversimplification is risky, but in an attempt to show why we do the things we do, examining the way the two hemispheres of your brain function can be very, very helpful.

Each side of the brain processes information differently

and has its own specialization, although at any given time you are using both sides of your brain. It's more a matter of emphasis than exclusivity. Still, we refer to linear thinkers as left-brain or logic-brain people. Right-brainers (artistic brain) tend to be more creative, visual, and emotional, although mathematical ability is located in the right brain also. The right-brain person is a divergent thinker in a one-track world, and at times this can be a struggle.

Nearly all the time management products on the market favor the left-brain thinking style, ignoring the needs of right-brainers. There's a simple reason for this: If you want to set up one system that's going to work for a lot of people, you're going to set up a left-brain system. Left-brainers learn patterns better, follow directions better, are better at details than right-brainers—and they're more alike. Right-brainers would prefer to concoct their own unique time-management tools (which is a great idea, by the way) rather than conform to an existing system.

Each style is incompatible with the other, and the creative will quickly discount or discard a rigid time management system. Some of the skills that are second nature for the left-brained person are awkward and difficult for the right-brainer—and vice versa. Although you can't always do what comes naturally, you can't expect a completely unnatural system to work for you. The challenge is to find out where your strengths lie and take advantage of them. Better than that, strive for a whole-brain (lateralized) approach to time management, organization—and life.

ABOUT THE RIGHT-BRAINER

The triumph over anything is a matter of organization.

—Kurt Vonnegut

You can do as much as your left-brain counterpart (maybe more) but prefer to do it in your own unique way. With a little savoir faire. Despite the negative bias against right-brainers as unproductive, undisciplined dreamers, you can get things done and have fun, too.

The right brain is artistic (can draw and paint), intuitive (perceptive and receptive to hunches), rhythmic (can see and feel patterns), fun (spontaneous, with a keen sense of humor), visual (nonverbal), spatial (it's the part that works jigsaw puzzles), nonjudgmental (sees and accepts different points of view), imaginative (creative and makes odd associations), metaphorical (uses imagery), emotional (people oriented and empathetic), holistic (sees the big picture), divergent (deals well with more than one thing at a time), sexual (just thought you'd like to know that), nonlinear (prefers to jump around rather than follow a step-by-step approach), illogical, irrational, and persuasive, too. It's also the site of the unconscious mind (where dreams reside).

As a right-brainer, you are unique. You may also be unpredictable, impatient, sloppy, and offbeat. You may loath routines, lack follow-through, abhor structure and rules, take a wait-and-see approach more often than not, juggle several tasks at once, and deal well with change, whether you want to or not. Organizing comes naturally to you, but not organizing that anybody else might recognize as such. You want to have fun; are freewheeling rather than focused, a day-dreamer; your train of thought tends to wane and wander; you're oblivious of time. You learn with visual clues, are impulsive, a risk taker. Being nonlinear, you find lists a little confining and tidiness a waste of time. You're independent, artistic, tend to ramble from topic to topic, speak with feeling, are easily distracted, lose things easily and frequently, can see the big picture but have trouble with individual steps, are indecisive, easygoing, and all too flexible. Dramatic and animated, you're a flirt, drive too fast, often speak without thinking, think well on your feet, and, did I mention, you are wonderful!

ABOUT THE LEFT-BRAINER

We are born princes, and the civilizing process makes us frogs.

—*Eric Berne*

The left hemisphere of your brain is the timekeeper (linear awareness), logical (just the facts, please), analytical (good with relationships, abstractions), linear (prefers a sequential, step-by-step approach), critical (judgmental), verbal (language and speech and spelling), compartmentalized (likes to do things one at a time, keeps home and work separate). It's also the center of memory (names but not faces).

People who are left-brain dominant are often good at researching and retaining information, fact gathering, math, tidiness, and written instructions. They may be willing to work long hours but consider work and play two separate things. They are responsible, good at organizing, obsessive, compulsive, dislike change, are easily overloaded, a little on the dull side, into conformity, controlling, very judgmental, and insensitive at times. They can be strong finishers; focused; perfectionists; detail oriented; goal oriented; list makers; orderly and stable; good with scheduling, repetition, and routine; punctual; decisive; uptight, fearful, and cautious. We need them to keep things running smoothly, to read the manuals and fix what we broke.

I often wonder if the left brain wasn't designed just to keep the right brain in line, the voice of reason. It sets the rules (and tries to make the right side adhere to them). It drives you toward consistency, toward timeliness, toward productiveness. "Chop, chop!" it will say. "In a minute!" the right will say. It's up to you to keep them from fighting.

THE WHOLE BRAIN

The chief function of your body is to carry your brain around.

—Thomas Edison

You should have recognized some of yourself in the descriptions of both right- and left-brainers. There's a lot of overlap in function, and the balance can vary at different times during your life. It's sort of like having Captain Kirk (right brain) and Mr. Spock (left brain) in your head at the same time. They argue sometimes—but when they work together, there's no world they can't conquer. Captain Picard, by the way, is a fully evolved whole-brain thinker.

Neither side is better or worse, right or wrong. Both hemispheres interact constantly, and you shift back and forth all day long depending on what you're doing. If you have a dominant side, however, your approach to a given problem will reflect that perspective.

Tapping into the full resources of your brain—both right and left sides—gives you the best of both worlds. Using both hemispheres of the brain to their full capacity is the goal. The right-brained artist who can do simple accounting and make it to meetings on time has an advantage, as does the left-brained accountant who can find alternative (legal) approaches to a knotty tax problem. A healthy balance between the two halves of the brain leads to more creativity and productivity. When the two halves work in harmony (rather than bickering back and forth), you also have inner peace.

As a drummer, I recognize the advantages of a whole-brain approach. Besides the obvious benefit of being able to manage all your extremities doing different things simultaneously, it is also good to have rhythm, emotion, and spontaneity when playing (right brain) as well as being able to read music, focus, and maintain a sense of time (left brain.) The two hemispheres complement each other and work in concert with each other.

Motor Skills

Your body is controlled by opposite sides of your brain. For instance: Put your left foot in (that's your right brain), put your right foot out (that's your left brain), do the hokey-pokey (that's your right brain again—you know, the side having all the fun), and shake it all about.

DIFFERENT STROKES

Success rests with having the courage and endurance and above all the will to become the person you are, however peculiar that may be. Then you will be able to say, "I have found my hero and he is me."

—*Dr. George Sheehan*

Now that you have discovered which hemisphere of your brain dominates your behavior, let me just take a minute to point out how this manifests itself into a particular organizing style. How you manage your time is partly determined by the side of the brain you use most (as well as by environment and individual situation). There is no right or wrong way to do things, only better and best (with a few exceptions).

Here is a brief and partial listing of the diverse (and creative) approaches to time management used by the creative person:

SWITCHBOARD OPERATOR. Most comfortable when you have several things going on simultaneously, like to switch back and forth between projects, and welcome interruptions with glee. Sometimes have a problem with finishing what you start.

PILER. Preferring to pile rather than file, you use a "pile" cabinet system (pile things on top of the cabinet rather than inside) for fear that if you put it away, you'll never find it again. Sometimes have a problem finding things anyway and often have a problem finding things quickly.

HEAD CASE. You refuse to write anything down. You're starting to forget things, your brain is cluttered, and nobody else knows what you're doing; but other than that, no problems.

LAST-MINUTE JUNKIE. You like the excitement of waiting till the last minute. And it is exciting, except when you miss deadlines and eventually burn out on one too many all-nighters.

ALL OR NOTHING. You will get a burst of energy and work like crazy until you run out of steam. The big problem with this one (not to be negative) is that you tend not to accomplish anything until that energy boost comes along. When it does, you'd better finish the project while you're rolling, or you likely never will. Another aspect of this style is the creative who looks at a job and, if it can't be done in one fell swoop, won't attempt it at all.

JACK OF ALL TRADES. You know a lot about a lot of things, like new challenges and new stimuli. Problems arise when you change careers like underwear, can't focus for more than a minute at a time, and never develop a complete understanding of any one subject.

PACK RAT. You save everything, because everything is handy, potentially useful, or sentimental. This is costly in time, money, and energy when carried to extremes.

PREDICTABLY UNPREDICTABLE. Wild! Nobody ever knows what to expect next from you. You do what feels right at the time, but you never stop long enough to figure out what you really want out of life and could be going nowhere fast.

SNEAKY. There are some people who like to sneak up on things, poke holes in it, and work on it when their muse shows up. Although you may make a dent in it, you may also miss a deadline or need a lot of prodding to finish. Another type of sneaky character (sounds worse than it is) is the low-profiler—you know who you are. You keep quiet so nobody interferes with you, but you also never get the recognition you deserve.

PSYCHIC FRIEND. Very in touch with your intuitive side, which you use to advance your art, make decisions, and plan your day. This style works great if you buddy up with someone who can help with the details and the business end of things.

INSTIGATORS. Idea people who hate follow-through and details, you would much rather come up with the idea than carry it out. Even think-tankers have to deal with some follow-through, however. Your ideas are apt to be incomplete and unworkable if you don't deal with implementation on some level.

FREEWHEELER. You're a "good-time Charlie," fun to be around, spontaneous, impulsive, with a shoot-from-the-hip style. A little dose of advance planning and forethought could save you a lot of time and heartache. It could also help with that boredom and lack-of-focus problem you've been having.

NO-SHOW. You're forgetful, frequently late (a poor judge of time), and known as "difficult" to work with. You are caught up in your own world and lack respect for others' time and agendas. Needless to say, this style has a tremendous downside—namely unemployment.

THE BUSY BEAVER. You're always busy but never seem to get anything important done. There's nothing for this but discipline. Left brain, come on down! Learn how to focus and put first things first.

PIG PEN. "Why should I clean up when I'm just going to use it again tomorrow?" you argue. In the meantime, you leave a trail of clutter in your wake. You seem to thrive on chaos, but your health and your relationships are suffering.

BENDABLE BUDDY. You try to please everyone, so people often walk all over you, taking advantage of your generosity and your time. You'll drop everything to help a friend, take a call, or pitch in at work. Unfortunately, if you don't learn how to say "no," you will never get your own needs met or your own work done.

STRADDLER. Indecisive. Fearful. You're good at understanding options but have a difficult time making choices. So you straddle the fence, hoping the problem will work itself out or go away. You flip-flop on decisions that you do make and are known as wishy-washy (a Pisces trait, for all you astrology fans out there).

LONE RANGER. The perfectionist. You try to do everything yourself. There comes a point when delegating some portion of the work or "letting it go" is the only way to get ahead (and finish). People will like you better. Honest.

HYPERSENSITIVE. You don't take rejection or criticism well, so you procrastinate and hold yourself back, unwilling to risk the judgment of others. You tend to focus on the negative instead of learning from your mistakes.

It doesn't matter if you don't fit into one of the above profiles. The point is that there are as many individual styles as there are people—and a solution to the time management and organization problems of each personality.

TIME MANAGEMENT MYTHS

The function of the creative artist consists of making laws, not in following laws already made.
—Ferruccio Busoni

"Pick up those piles." "Put away those papers." "Post-it notes are bad." (Post-it notes are bad? That's it. This is war.) As a creative person, certainly you have heard these statements or others like them from time to time. It's time to debunk some of the mantras from the classic time management books—join in wherever you like.

TIME IS MONEY. Uh, time is more valuable than money, don't you think? And you should be more careful about how you spend your time and whom you give it away to. The only way to get more, unfortunately, is to save it, budget it, and hoard it for your most important needs.

PILES ARE BAD. Every piece of paper not in use at this moment should be in a file, because otherwise it will get lost. Hmm.

The truth is it doesn't matter whether you file or pile or spindle or sit on your papers. What matters is being able to find what you want, when you want it. Period.

A MESSY DESK IS A SIGN OF A MESSY MIND. Your desk is your own territory. As long as you're comfortable, it's nobody else's business how you run it.

AN EMPTY IN-BOX IS THE GOAL. Not everything needs to be done the minute it arrives. That's a bureaucrat's mistake. It is more important to do the key things and leave lesser tasks in the in-box or delegate them.

YOU SHOULD TRY TO DO THE MOST IN THE LEAST AMOUNT OF TIME. I personally think it's better to take the time to do a job right than just to get the job done. That's why time management became so important to me. I had to find that time somewhere.

TECHNOLOGY WILL HELP YOU DO IT BETTER, FASTER. Technology can speed up mundane, repetitive tasks. It can't speed up a creative mind. In fact, there's a strong argument that says you shouldn't try to speed up creativity. You lose more than you gain.

SET YOUR PRIORITIES AND STICK WITH THEM. Except priorities change, day by day, sometimes minute by minute, and certainly week by week. What world are these people living in?

A CLEAN, STERILE ENVIRONMENT IS BEST FOR THE WORKPLACE. For a doctor, yes, but not for the creative person. Pablo Picasso was on his porch one day, looking around his yard, when he spotted an old rusted bike leaning against a tree. He noticed that the handlebars resembled the horns of a bull. So he removed the handlebars from the bike and took them into his studio, where he created a sculpture of a charging bull. Clutter can be inspiring.

FOLLOW ROUTINES TO GET MORE DONE. It can be better to use your internal clock to tell you when to do what. Routines stifle creativity and spontaneity—you stop thinking and just act by reflex.

DO ONE THING AT A TIME. This is a real creativity stunter. You need to keep working that multilevel brain of yours in order to keep it working for you. Besides, you'd go broke if you did only one thing at a time.

HANDLE PAPER ONLY ONCE. An impossible and unnecessary rule. Sometimes going through papers, sorting your piles, sifting your words can give you inspiration, can energize you, can touch you. If you were going to handle paper only once, you'd toss everything (and even the leftiest left-brainers don't do that).

IF YOU HAVEN'T USED IT IN A YEAR, TOSS IT. (That's cold, man.) There are a lot of things that really do come in handy someday, and then there are all those things you save for the memories. Just be selective.

FILE EVERYTHING. "Have you seen the dog?" "Yeah, I filed him under *V* for *Veterinary*. Or was it *A* for *Animal husbandry? P* for *just Peed in the house?* Anyhow, I filed him."

GET MORE DONE AND YOU'LL BE HAPPIER. No, you'll just get more done.

CREATIVITY

Creativity is a highfalutin' word for the work I have to do between now and Tuesday.

—*David Ogilvy*

Ideas can come from anywhere at any time. A blouse blowing in the wind, billboards, old projects, memories, travel, free association. Pay attention to life. Pluck flowers from your experiences and create a beautiful bouquet.

Creativity is making new connections from existing things. A toy designer buttoning her daughter's blouse notices a balloon button, and an idea for a new design hits her. You meet a friend for drinks, and the mirror behind the bar gives you an idea for a design you're working on. While waiting in the doctor's office, you thumb through a ten-year-old magazine and get an idea for a new dress design. Ray Bradbury says swimming helps him come up with ideas, Charles Shultz plays tennis, and Steve Allen's best song ideas come to him in his sleep.

Press your nose to the window of life! Creativity is a gift, a unique way of seeing the world. But it's been clearly shown that you can lose your capacity for creativity if you repress it, if you don't use it. This book is about time management and organizing your life. Not so you can do more, but so you can *be* more.

2

• • • • •

TIME WELL SPENT

Love is life . . . and if you miss love, you miss life.
— *Leo Buscaglia*

When you rush around all day every day playing catch-up, without the time or resources to do your best work, you tend to fall into patterns, repeating the same safe formulas over and over—which may make your left-brained boss happy but could lead to loss of self-esteem, depression, and stunting of your natural talents.

Creative people need time to create, time to let ideas percolate, time to look around and find new images, learn new techniques, try on new styles. Originality does not follow a time clock, although *you* often have to. It's frustrating when your boss or client demands a logo or original art or brilliant copy—and have it ready tomorrow morning.

The problem is complex, but the answer is (relatively) simple. You must organize your time so that you get done the things that must be done, you arrive at your meetings on time and prepared, you don't neglect your family or your life—and you have time to be creative. Not time left over. There *is* no leftover time. But time scheduled just for you, for fun, for "percolating."

It is possible to build this time into your life and your lifestyle, but it can't be done haphazardly. You have to think about what truly needs to be done and dump the stuff that gets in the way. Don't tell me you're too busy to plan. If you don't plan, you'll be busy without accomplishing much and without realizing the fulfillment you need as a creative person. You don't have to go so fast if you're going in the right direction—and then you have time to enjoy the ride.

If this sounds too "left brained," too hard, too nerdy, think again. The most successful creative people have learned to set goals, schedule, and organize. They've learned it in self-defense. You've read about more than one famous actor who had wealth, power, and prestige yet died alone of a drug overdose; industrialists who spent their lives climbing the corporate ladder, sacrificing family and friends, only to have it taken away by a hostile takeover. Many apparently successful people spend all their time doing what they are told, only to realize that they missed the chance to fulfill their own dreams.

Creative people need to make time to "let it out." Unable to create, you become angry, resentful, frustrated, and unhappy. You also need to take time to recharge. Creativity is fragile; if you don't nurture it, it can die, leaving you recycling old ideas and pretending they're fresh. It's a sure road to mediocrity.

A friend of mine works as a graphic artist for a publication made up entirely of ads. His job is to design the ads as quickly as possible. He admits that he could live with the long hours and low pay; the fact that he doesn't have time to be creative bothers him a lot, however. He's bored and frustrated, his ads all look alike, and he's facing burnout with nothing to show for it.

You don't have to live like that. There are other ways to deal with—and avoid—burnout. Be honest with yourself Mike Myers took some time off after the success of the *Wayne's World* movies because, as he says, "I was tired, and you can't be very funny or creative when you're tired."

I once knew the producer of a hit TV show in Los Angeles. She should have been on top of the world; her show was a ratings leader, and she was making money hand over fist. The problem was that all she ever did was work. She had no time for a relationship and found that it was lonely at the top. She became bored once the show was established, and each episode began to look pretty much the same. She was no longer creating anything, and she felt guilty about being paid so well. Finally she moved away from Hollywood to a sleepy coastal town and began pursuing other interests (while still maintaining the role of part-time producer). She made less money, lived in a smaller home, had less say in producing the show, but ultimately she was happier.

Are you so busy working that you're unable to enjoy your work or the fruits of your labor? In the marina where I keep my boat, there are several big, beautiful yachts that sit unused for years at a time because the owners are too busy to go sailing.

You need time off. The old rule "Work hard now and play later" doesn't apply to you. Sure, you should work hard, but for you, work is life. You must spend time enjoying both, without any guilt. (I know, try explaining this to your boss.)

The creative brain is triggered by the senses (sight, smell, taste, touch, and sound). That's why it is time well spent to get out, to get away from the office, to break your normal routine and look around you. Bill Bowerman, the man who invented Nike shoes, was dawdling through breakfast one morning when he noticed his wife's waffle iron. He realized a waffle pattern would give shoe soles better traction—and the rest is history.

You need to experience life in order to be creative; if you don't experience people, places, and things, your art and your life will become stagnant.

"But I don't have time," "But I'm on deadline," "But there just aren't enough hours in the day." I've heard it all before—I've made the same rationalizations. The first thing you have to do is dump the excuses. They just get in the way of recognizing the important things, setting realistic priorities, and creating the life you want to be living. If you didn't need to get past the excuses and find a way to make your life work for you, you wouldn't be reading this book. I'll help, but you've got to do it.

THE SOLUTION

Our life is frittered away by detail. . . . Simplify.
Simplify.

—Henry David Thoreau

Effective time management means having time left over to do the things you want to do. It gives you time to spend with family and friends, to be creative and to enjoy life. This time is not given to you. You must take it.

Good time management affords you time to be spontaneous without the guilt. It allows you to take the long way home, to daydream, to socialize, and to pursue those things that bring you the most joy and happiness.

Good time management also means not always being frazzled with unneeded stress and anxiety. It allows you to take fun breaks and recharge. You will have time to stop and smell the flowers. Enjoy the process.

Creativity is an asset in the nineties. The truly creative person has far more opportunities in nearly every field and is generally regarded as special. In order to take advantage of the edge nature has given you, however, you must learn to develop your potential, nurture your talent, and use your time wisely.

ALL WORK AND NO PLAY

Life is about opening yourself up to possibilities.
That's what life is about.

—Oprah Winfrey

Society tends to reward obsessive-compulsive behavior; many managers won't recognize that you're working unless you're slaving away at your desk. You may find yourself working many long hours trying to escape something you're afraid to face. You may binge on adrenaline highs and love living in a constant state of crisis—to the point where you create a crisis if one isn't handy. You may be addicted to accomplishments, moving from one to the next without taking time to recharge or bask in the glow of your achievements.

You may have gotten away with this kind of behavior so far, but you already could be suffering some consequences—and eventually you'll burn out. The problems you may face include drug and alcohol addiction, health problems, divorce, and depression.

● ●

Are You a Workaholic?

Before you answer, take the test below. You may be surprised by your answers.

(Answer yes or no)

❏ YES ❏ NO **1.** Was your last vacation more than twelve months ago?

❏ TES ❏ NO **2.** Do you hate the thought of going to work every morning?

❏ YES ❏ NO **3.** In the last six months, has nobody told you that you work too much?

❏ YES ❏ NO **4.** Do you often take work home with you?

❏ YES ❏ NO **5.** Do you regularly work late and/or work weekends?

❏ YES ❏ NO **6.** Do you feel tired and restless on Monday morning?

❏ YES ❏ NO **7.** Is poor health affecting your work?

❏ YES ❏ NO **8.** Is your work always on your mind, even during time off?

❏ YES ❏ NO **9.** Have you changed the oil in your car in the past six months?

❏ YES ❏ NO **10.** Have your pets forgotten who you are?

❏ YES ❏ NO **11.** Have you canceled plans with your family or friends in the past six months in order to get more work done?

☐ YES ☐ NO **12.** Do you go from one project to the next without a break?

☐ YES ☐ NO **13.** Do you feel overworked and underpaid?

☐ YES ☐ NO **14.** Do alcohol, coffee, cigarettes, and so on help you handle the pressures of work?

☐ YES ☐ NO **15.** Do you feel guilty if you take time just to goof off?

☐ YES ☐ NO **16.** Has it been more than six months since you last did something for yourself?

☐ YES ☐ NO **17.** Have you sacrificed your personal life or goals for your work?

☐ YES ☐ NO **18.** Has your personal life suffered as a result of your work?

☐ YES ☐ NO **19.** Do you tend to take on too much at once and miss deadlines or leave projects unfinished as a result?

☐ YES ☐ NO **20.** When was the last time you slept late?

☐ YES ☐ NO **21.** Do you get an adrenaline high from working under the gun and having a lot going on?

☐ YES ☐ NO **22.** Do you have a hard time getting started before the time pressure is intense?

☐ YES ☐ NO **23.** Are you committed to projects into the next millennium with no end in sight?

☐ YES ☐ NO **24.** Are your weekends busy, busy, busy?

☐ YES ☐ NO **25.** Do you feel obligated to do a lot of things you don't want to do?

☐ YES ☐ NO **26.** Are you out of touch with the latest movies, plays, music?

Answer "yes" to more than eight of these, and you qualify as a workaholic. It's time to reorganize your life.

• •

WHERE DOES ALL YOUR TIME GO?

Slow down and enjoy life. It's not only the scenery you miss by going too fast—you also miss the sense of where you are going and why.

—*Eddie Cantor*

Have you ever stopped to try to figure out where your time goes? Of course not—who has the time?

I know people say time stops for no man and that it speeds up as we get older. I would have said that was baloney a few years back, but it does seem as if time has started slipping past me lately. One way I notice this is each Sunday when I pull the TV listings out of the paper. It feels as though just yesterday I set the old one on the coffee table.

Here is a quick look at why you never seem to have enough time to do the things you want to do.

• •

Time Sharks (Things That Eat into Your Time)

Number of hours in one week: 168 (7 days x 24 hours = 168)

EXAMPLE OF AN AVERAGE PERSON (IN HOURS)			You
Eating:	14	(2 hrs. per day)	____
Sleeping:	56	(8 hrs. per night)	____
Bathroom:	5	(Includes shower time)	____
Working:	45	(8 hrs. x 5 days + overtime)	____
Commuting:	10	(2 hr. per day x 5 days)	____
Exercising:	3	(1 hr. 3 days per week)	____
Shopping:	2	(Groceries, etc.)	____
Errands:	1	(Other than shopping)	____
Cleaning:	1	(Other than yourself)	____
Meetings:	1	(Other than work)	____
Paying Bills:	.5	(It must be done)	____
Phone Calls:	3.5	(30 min. per day x 7 days)	____
TV:	14	(Includes TV news)	____
Other:	7	(Kids, classes, misc.)	____

Total Time Used: 163
Time Left Over: 5   (This is your "free" time)

●●●●●●●●●●●●●●●●●●●●●●●●●●●●●●●●

HOW TO FIND THE TIME

You will never find time for anything. If you want time, you must take it.

—*Charles Burton*

Schedule "personal time" on your calendar first, then set up appointments and block out work hours. Include time for rest and relaxation, socializing, time with your family, and time needed to create. Stick to your calendar. Keep it with you, and don't book more than one thing in an hour, preferably no more than two scheduled items each half day. This should help keep you from overbooking yourself with all that "other" stuff you feel you must do. Other ways to "find" time include the following:

- Are there people in your life who have no respect for your time? People who are always asking you to do this or that for them or who stop by to chat frequently and to no purpose? List these people, write down their names. Then limit the time you spend with them. Practice saying, "I'm sorry, I'm busy just now." Your time is a precious commodity. Don't let others squander it.

- Consciously decide that everybody doesn't have to like you. Let's face it: you can't please everyone all the time, so you might as well please yourself. Remember that every "yes" to someone who needs a piece of your time is a "no" to something that you may want to do for yourself or those you care about. Don't waffle. Be polite but firm. Expect to surprise people at first, but most will respect you. Those who can't adjust to your newfound authority are better off out of your social circle anyway.

- Look for things you can combine to save time and accomplish more. Meet a friend at the gym and work out together rather than hanging out at a bar. Go for a walk with your spouse or significant other, spending some quality time together while walking the dog and getting your exercise all at the same time. How about reading the paper or watching the news while you ride the exercise bike? Listen to books on tape while you commute.

- If you are constantly stuck in traffic going to work, waiting in line for lunch, or waiting to use the weights at the gym after work, think about working a swing shift. Come in early or start a little later to avoid the traffic, take lunch at off hours, and work out while everyone else is still in the office. Working off hours also lets you pursue hobbies that require daylight time or are subject to nature. I go surfing every morning, which means I don't start my workday until ten A.M. But I make sure I'm at my desk ready to work at ten A.M.

A woman I know who lives close to her office goes in at eleven A.M., turns in projects, makes contacts, and gets information she needs. At four P.M. she goes home, takes a break and eats an early dinner, then goes back to the office from seven to eleven P.M. and gets a ton of work done in the quiet of a deserted office. It's a nine-hour day, but she claims it's not as tiring as a nine A.M. to five P.M. schedule, and all of her time is productive. She's happy, her boss is happy, and she's gotten very close to a cute security guard.

If you don't think your company will allow skewed hours—ask anyway. If you can show an increase in productivity, they might just make an exception in your case.

- Get up an hour early to paint, write, read, or work on your own personal project. It's a great way to start the day, especially if your job doesn't provide a creative outlet.

- If you have a big project that you must get done, ignore the mail, the phone, and the laundry until you finish what you have to do. I call this "having a hack attack." Concentrate on your project with the knowledge that you will catch up on all those things you let slip when you finish. Ask yourself, What is the worst thing that can happen if I postpone these other things temporarily? If you can live with the worst thing, then postponing is okay. This is called *prioritizing*. (Don't be afraid of that word. Prioritizing is your friend.)

Do *not* postpone your family time, breaks, personal time, meals, and sufficient sleep. If the project is so big that it eats into this, you either need to delegate parts of it, extend the deadline to a realistic time frame, or break it up into smaller pieces that you can handle while having a life.

- Are you as efficient as you can be? Apply the 80/20 rule to how your time is spent. For instance, the rule says that 80 percent of your sales comes from 20 percent of your customers, 80 percent of your production comes from 20 percent of your workday. What do you do during the unproductive 80 percent of your day? Find out.

We're talking about working smarter. Nanci McGraw labels that less than productive time as "milking the mouse" in her book *Organized for Success*. A task or project that takes a lot of time and effort for very little return is like milking a mouse. Examples are doing a task you could easily delegate; obsessing about a task; taking too long to complete a task; starting a task before you have all the relevant information; or doing a task like untangling paper clips that keeps you from doing something more important.

- Being more efficient with paperwork is a prime example of squeezing extra time out of a day. Having a system to deal with paperwork—or better yet, someone to help with it—can really add time to your day. As a creative person, filling out forms and submitting reports will rarely be the best use of your time. Why not get help? Do what you do best and delegate the rest.

- If you find it impossible to find large blocks of time, use whatever free time you do have. When I am on the road giving all-day seminars, I will spend my lunchtime going for a swim in the pool or finding a quiet place to read a good book. I need this time to be alone and recharge.

- Stock up and save time. Keep basic supplies like stamps, envelopes, and the like ready for when you need them. Buy in bulk. Save for a rainy day.

- Set some rules to ensure that you take time to have fun or spend with loved ones. For instance, you may say no work and no business calls after six P.M. and no work on weekends.

- Let it go. If you are a perfectionist and use up time trying to make sure everything is absolutely perfect, try letting go of the things that really don't matter. If you spend an hour creating and designing a new "things to do" list and then spend another thirty minutes making sure it prints perfectly, you're wasting time.

Think about what you're doing. Rate its importance in the grand scheme of your life. This is not a complain-about-how-full-your-life-is-of-time-consuming-garbage exercise. This is another prioritizing point. I know a graphic artist who says, "I spend the same amount of time on a $150 job as I do on a $500 job. I guess I need to get more $500 jobs." Wrong! What she needs to do is spend $150 worth of time on $150 jobs, then let it go.

LIVING IN THE MOMENT

You only live once, but if you work it right, once is enough.

—Joe E. Lewis

If you take time off, do you really enjoy it? Or are you still thinking about work? Worse still, do you bring work with you on vacations?

In the movie *Vacation,* starring Chevy Chase, Chase's character and family travel across the country and finally arrive at the Grand Canyon. As the Griswold family comes to the edge of the canyon, Chase's character looks over the edge and says, "Okay, we've seen it. Let's go." Obviously he is missing the point, but at least he made it to the canyon and, eventually, Wally World. My uncle never went. He'd seen the diorama at Disneyland and figured that was as good as the real thing. It isn't.

In the past, I came home from vacations more tired than when I left. I was always trying to fit some work in. I never really took the time to just enjoy; I just had to complete this project or make that important call. This kind of attitude vitiates all the benefits of taking time off.

Here are a few tips on how to live in the moment and get the most out of your "free" time:

- **Don't wear a watch** while on vacation.
- **Leave your pager** and cellular phone at home.
- **Do what you want,** when you want. It feels great.
- **Don't read business books** on days off.
- **Finish your project** before you go. If you can't get it done, let it go and deal with it when you get back. In either case, put it out of your mind. You'll have a fresher approach when you return.
- **Don't take on any new projects** within a week of leaving for vacation—no matter how small, how simple, how "only you can do this" they may be.
- **Get together with old friends** who are not in the same industry as you so you won't be tempted to talk about work.
- **Get as far away from it all as you can**—physically and mentally. Get away from the phone, the office, the boss, clients, your familiar surroundings.

Fast Fact

A survey conducted by the Boston Market Food Chain revealed that 54 percent of Americans take less than a half hour for lunch and that 37 percent take less than fifteen minutes. The survey also found that 79 percent of those questioned said they were more productive after a good lunch and 60 percent said they were more positive about work after a good lunch.

So, to improve your productivity, take a long lunch.

FOOD FOR THOUGHT

The secret of happiness is not found in seeking more, but in developing the capacity to enjoy less.
                                    —*Dan Millman*

Drew Silvern, thirty-four years old and single, worked as a writer for the *San Diego Union-Tribune* newspaper. He enjoyed spending time with Beasley, his pet Labrador retriever—and he was dying of cancer. Since he was first diagnosed with a brain tumor, and throughout his treatment, he wrote about his ordeal. His words are both painful and revealing. Like many cancer patients, Silvern discovered what a gift life is and how short it can be.

"There are days when I wake up, strap on my portable CD player, and walk Beasley for an hour along Sunset Cliffs, he wrote. "Often, I feel an indescribable joy that I'm able to do this. It's a cancer dividend, and I always offer a prayer of thanksgiving at the midpoint. In my first life (before being diagnosed with cancer), the morning walk would probably have been just another thing to get done before work. Cancer has given me a raw appreciation for life I'm sure I never would have felt without it.

"In a way, my cancer came along at the worst possible

time, and maybe the best. It made the past the past and the present the present. It healed most of the old scars and propelled me beyond regret or family resentments. It brought clarity of purpose to my life and a sudden ability to see the glass as half full."

● ●

Balancing Act

Do you lead a balanced life? On the following chart put a dot where you feel you fall for each of the following categories. Then connect the dots and analyze what you spend the bulk of your time doing and whether you lead a balanced life.

TIME	WORKING	SOCIAL/FUN	EXERCISE	FAMILY	SELF/LEARNING	TV/BAD HABITS	OTHER
Most							
Lots							
Some							
Not Enough							
None							

● ●

TIME WELL SPENT IS . . .

I like to drive with my knees. Otherwise, how can I put on my lipstick and talk on the phone?

—*Sharon Stone*

I'll give you my personal definition of time well spent:

STOPPING TO SMELL THE FLOWERS. This means taking time away from work and time "away" during work. If necessary, put off buying that new car in favor of a much needed vacation. Turn off the TV. Don't allow yourself to say you'll start enjoying life as soon as . . . Do it now! By setting priorities, getting clear with yourself about what and who is important, you can avoid getting caught up in the frenzy of everyday life.

Once you learn to say "no," to focus on the things that matter to you, your life will never be the same. (It will be better.)

TAKING THE LONG WAY HOME. Literally. Instead of rushing to get home from work, take the scenic route and enjoy the view. By breaking up the monotony of familiar habits, you can gain a refreshingly new perspective on things. Steven Spielberg says his best ideas have come to him while he was driving through Los Angeles. A good, long road trip can be therapeutic as well. Use the time alone to collect your thoughts and to reflect on what's working and what isn't. The simple act of driving can even trigger new and creative solutions brought on by the visual and tactile stimuli.

TAKING FREQUENT BREAKS. You will be much more productive and creative if you take a ten-minute break for every hour you work. (I know, try telling this to your employer/client/supervisor.) But it's true. There comes a point of diminishing returns when you continue to push yourself without taking a break. In the long run, a short digression from a project or task will renew and invigorate you, and you'll be more productive and creative during the time you are working. This could mean something as simple as getting up and stretching or playing a (short) game on your computer.

MIXING IT UP. Variety is the spice of life for creative types. Don't fight your natural tendency to flit from one task to another. Use this to your advantage to stay fresh. Most creative types abhor repetitive work yet are able to handle several things at once. This is an asset. When you find yourself bored with one task, break the monotony and move on to something else. When you return to the original task, you may well return with renewed energy and creativity.

TAKING TIME TO RECHARGE AND REGROUP. You must defend your need for time to do nothing. Without it, you will lose your creative edge—often becoming angry, tense, unhappy, or depressed. You may prefer to finish a project at the last minute by working through the night. That's okay, as long as you take a little time off before moving on to something new. You need time to "unmind."

The time you spend replenishing your energy supply is time well spent. Author Brian Tracy suggests that highly successful people aren't sure whether their car radios work. Why? Because whenever they are in their cars they are listening to self-help tapes. As much as I admire Brian Tracy, I feel this is overkill. It's okay to relax to music after a tough day at work. In fact, I strongly encourage you to do it.

VOLUNTEERING YOUR TIME TO HELP OTHERS. Using your creativity to make a positive impact is one of the most fulfilling feelings there is. Just don't give till it hurts. Be wary of losing yourself in a cause at the expense of your own well-being.

TAKING TIME TO PUTTER. Puttering about the garage or in the kitchen can be an excellent stress reliever. Fiddling with an ongoing project (which has no deadline for completion) can enhance your creativity and take your mind off your work, at least for a few hours. During this time you may even gain a valuable new insight into how to tackle that problem.

If you don't have a hobby outside of what you do for a living, get one. If you have a hobby but never seem to find the time to pursue it anymore, make the time. Do something for no other reason than that it gives you a pure sense of joy. If you feel guilty about this fun time, involve your kids, spouse, friends, or even your clients.

TIME WITH FAMILY AND FRIENDS. Close relationships with family and friends can be vital to your stability. Some religions feel that family life "grounds" a person and is essential simply for that purpose. Yet this is the first place most people cut time from when they get busy with work. Your spouse, your kids—heck, even your pet needs and wants quality time with you, and you need them. A healthy relationship with your family and friends requires time and attention. A word of caution: Don't waste your time with people who try to bring you down or are a negative influence. (Go ahead and burn that bridge.) Time spent with those who support and genuinely care about your happiness is an investment in your own well-being.

Time with family also includes regular calls to your mom

and dad, grandparents, and siblings. There is no substitute for the unconditional love you get from (and give to) your family. It gives you a solid basis from which to face the rest of the world; it can give you confidence and encourage your own creativity. Don't neglect this area of your life, or one day you'll realize that you don't have a life at all.

TAKING TIME TO BE ALONE. Creative individuals need time alone; the amount of time you need will vary depending on your personality and situation. In general, the more stress you are under, the more time you need to be alone. This means more than closing the door to your office. Taking the long way home is a good way to get a daily dose of yourself. Walking or jogging are other ways to get inside yourself. In *The Artist's Way*, the authors call walking "moving meditation." Privacy and solitude allow your subconscious to send up all those creative ideas it's been working on while you were otherwise occupied.

I was asked recently when I felt totally at peace with myself. I was surprised when the two examples I came up with both involved being completely alone. The first was being alone on my boat with no particular destination, just cruising along the coast of California. The second was a road trip I took to Palm Springs. Instead of taking the freeway, I chose a longer, more tranquil route through the mountains. I was totally at peace as I meandered along the back roads of the mountains and desert, singing happily at the top of my lungs.

TIME OFF FOR GOOD BEHAVIOR. When was the last time you "got away from it all"? A real vacation means no work, no business calls, and sometimes no kids. When people are asked what they would do if they won a million dollars in the lottery, the most popular answer is always "Travel." What are you waiting for?

TAKING YOUR INNER CHILD OUT TO LUNCH. Every once in a while it's a good idea to take your inner child to lunch. If you have ever heard the words "You're acting like a child," then you're on the right track! The need to play is part of your internal makeup and requires occasional attention. This could mean dancing in the rain, playing catch with a buddy, making a sand castle with your kids, or just doing something goofy. Grow up, don't grow old.

TAKING A CATNAP. You'd be surprised how many people incorporate a nap into their daily routine. Famous and successful people use these "power napes" to recharge. Winston Churchill took daily naps, even during the height of World War II. Don't fight the tendency to close your eyes in the middle of the afternoon for a quick snooze. Be careful not to overdo it, though. Ten to twenty minutes is best. You'll wake up refreshed, recharged, and ready to take on the world.

TAKING TIME TO STAY FIT. Exercise creates a natural high and can increase your energy for the entire day. It helps you sleep better at night. A healthy body is necessary for the creative mind to function properly; don't neglect your physical self. Eat properly and exercise regularly. You know this already. *Doing* it's the kicker.

TAKING TIME TO DAYDREAM. Open up your mind and let it go. Explore new ideas—the process here is as important as any results. Exercise that mind, stretch it in new directions, try new approaches to old problems. Experiment. Try on different creative disciplines—writing, painting, sculpting, dancing. This is what creativity is all about.

DOING YOUR CHORES. Most time management books preach the gospel of hiring others to do things like washing the car, mowing the lawn, pulling weeds, folding the laundry, or cleaning out the garage. For the creative person, however, these menial tasks can be a respite, a break, a change of pace that's badly needed. And you can feel good about the concrete, visible fruits of your labor.

CURLING UP WITH A GOOD BOOK. A good book can take you to distant places away from work and other problems. I used to feel that reading a mystery or thriller was a waste of time. Was I ever wrong! I am still a voracious reader of nonfiction, but I no longer read these books when I want to relax. I finally learned how to read for fun.

TAKING THE TIME TO STAY CURRENT. Have you ever felt left out when a friend or co-worker made a joke based on the latest episode of the hit TV show you never have time to watch? Or when your date asks you if you like Hootie and the Blowfish and you reply that fish makes you sick? (It's a popular pop band, by the way.) When a neighbor wants to discuss the upcoming election and you can't even bluff your way through (you just hope he won't ask when you last voted)? Or when your best client wants to rehash the big game? It pays to spend a little time staying on top of trends—and not just for conversation's sake. As a creative person, it helps to stay in touch with what's hot and what's not.

NETWORKING. These days, who you know determines how far you'll go and how fast you'll get there. Networking isn't just a buzzword anymore, it's the way to get ahead in today's world. Being a good networker means taking the time to send thank-you notes, clipping and sending articles for colleagues, actively looking for ways to help those around you, and remembering birthdays and anniversaries. Networking takes time. It means going to lunch with a co-worker, meeting with a mentor, or attending an occasional cocktail party or break-fast club meeting. The payoff is having a network of people who like and respect you and want to reciprocate by helping you out when you need them most.

PRESSING THE FLESH. With the advent of faxes, e-mail, voice mail, and teleconferencing, who needs to actually talk to any-one anymore? You do. Nothing can replace a face-to-face meeting, a one-on-one sales call, or a brainstorming session with your team. It is also a good idea to set up breakfast or lunch dates with those you do business with.

GOING BACK TO SCHOOL. Classes, seminars, and workshops can put you back into a creative environment as well as teach you new concepts and skills. The energy you reap from being around others who are involved and interested is well worth the time and effort.

FLASHING FORWARD. A few minutes of advance planning can save you hours of time down the road. Instead of waiting until your car is running on fumes, fill up with gas when you get down to half a tank. This saves you from running out of gas, of course, and also from having to stop to fill up when you're already running a half hour late. Put what you need to take with you by the door with your car keys the night before you leave for work, a trip, or a meeting. That way you don't forget things and you don't waste time hunting for what you need when you're already running late in the morning.

Have you ever had the hard drive to your computer crash, wiping out months of work? Of course you took the time to back up all your files, right? If you have ever had this happen to you, as I did, it is all the wake-up call you need to start backing up all your files. Plan a regular time to back up your files—and do it.

● ●

Action Item

Make a list of the things you once enjoyed doing but haven't done in years. Or you never did but always wanted to. These are things like camping, painting, traveling, singing in a band, writing, snorkeling, Rollerblading, golf, basketball, reading, running, baking, horseback riding, biking, swimming, and so on. Now put one of these items in your calendar to do next week.

● ●

Time Well Spent Makeover

Below is an example of how you can go from chaos to control.

Before

07:00 A.M.	Alarm goes off, hit snooze button
07:15 A.M.	Wearily get out of bed
07:20 A.M.	Shower/get ready
07:45 A.M.	Dress in mail-order outfit that doesn't fit quite right. Hunt for shoes.
07:55 A.M.	Grab a quick breakfast and skim paper

08:05 A.M.	Look for lost keys (again)
08:10 A.M.	Start commute to work in boring but practical car
08:15 A.M.	Stop for gas
08:40 A.M.	Arrive at work (late again)
01:00 P.M.	Too busy to stop for lunch
04:00 P.M.	Just finished with urgent tasks
06:00 P.M.	Still at work finishing project due last week
06:30 P.M.	Stop at same old fast food, take-out restaurant
07:00 P.M.	Watch TV and eat dinner
09:30 P.M.	You are exhausted, so you go to bed

After

Alarm goes off, you get up	6:00 A.M.
Watch the sunrise as you go for a brisk walk	6:05 A.M.
Shower/get ready	6:35 A.M.
Put on new outfit that makes you feel great	7:00 A.M.
Grab your keys and things you put next to door	7:15 A.M.
Get in your convertible car with full tank of gas	7:20 A.M.
Beat rush-hour traffic with early start	7:30 A.M.
Stop at quaint café for breakfast and read paper	7:45 A.M.
Get early start at new job that you love	8:15 A.M.
Have a picnic lunch with a co-worker	12:00 P.M.
Close door, put on voice mail, and finish project	3:00 P.M.
Leave work in time to catch sunset/read book	5:15 P.M.
Stop at market to pick up fresh vegetables, chat with grocer	5:45 P.M.
Prepare a meal you've never tried before	6:00 P.M.
Take a relaxing bath	7:00 P.M.
Meet a friend for a movie	7:30 P.M.
Reflect on day and prepare for tomorrow	9:30 P.M.
Turn in with a good book, relaxed and refreshed	10:00 P.M.

IS YOUR CALENDAR FULL YET?

Many people take no care of their money till they come nearly to the end of it, and others do just the same thing with their time.

—Johann Wolfgang von Goethe

By this time, your calendar should be pretty full. I've listed a lot of things you need to do for yourself on top of your own regular work schedule. Even when you prioritize and dump the things you don't need or want to do, you may be wondering where you're going to find the time for all the rest. You're not going to find the time. You're going to make the time. Here's how:

- **Carry a notepad** or microrecorder so that if you come up with a great idea, you can jot it down or record it before you forget.

- **Reward yourself** after you have completed a big project or task with time off, a fun break, or a splurge.

- **Meet friends** or your spouse at the gym to combine two things. Involve your family in the business to stay close.

- **Find work that you love,** work that allows you to express your creativity and makes use of your talent. If you can't find fun work, make it fun, make it a game. By making work fun, you will need less time off. Attitude is everything. Make work fun by holding meetings outside or having pizza parties when a job is completed or while working late to finish a project. Softball teams, company picnics, and get-togethers all help build morale and make work fun.

  CAUTION: Too much play and not enough work can also be a problem. Don't take this too far. As always, moderation is the key. Time well spent doesn't mean goofing off instead of washing the dishes, calling clients, or meeting important deadlines. It means fitting fun into the framework of your personal and professional life.

- **Take advantage of little bits of free time.** Take several long weekends rather than one long vacation. If a meeting is canceled, use the "found" time to go to a matinee, catch a ball game, go swimming, go to the beach, and so on.

- **Commit one day a week to cutting loose.** Make a date with your mate. Make a date with yourself to do something alone. Maybe you can work a Saturday in order to get a Monday off to catch a game or take a road trip or pick up your kids from school and coach their soccer team.

- **When you really need time to think, to be alone, *take it*.** Do your work somewhere other than the office. Get away from the phone. Don't tell anyone where you are. Start work early or stay late.

- **Make up a list of affirmations** to read every morning that give you permission to play. They could include things like "It's okay to have fun," "I deserve to be paid well," "I deserve to take time off."

DO YOU GET IT?

The secret of life is enjoying the passage of time.
—*James Taylor*

After reading this chapter, which of the following would you consider to be time well spent?

❑ Taking the long way for a change of scenery

❑ Taking a ten-minute break every hour

❑ Taking a much needed vacation

❑ Listening to relaxing music

❑ Going to a ball game

❑ Reading a bedtime story to your kid

❑ Going to an art gallery

- ❏ Seeing the latest movie
- ❏ Backing up your computer files
- ❏ Pursuing a hobby
- ❏ Spending time with family and friends
- ❏ Taking an afternoon nap
- ❏ Daydreaming
- ❏ Trying a new approach to solve an old problem
- ❏ Exercising
- ❏ Taking a long walk alone
- ❏ Networking with clients and co-workers
- ❏ Sending thank-you notes
- ❏ Planning ahead

All of the above are good uses of your time. Take the ones you have checked and enter them into your calendar. If you schedule time for yourself, you'll have it. Otherwise it will dribble away.

Remember, when anyone asks you to do something, refer to your calendar to see if you have time. If you don't, say "no" politely but firmly. If you do, ask yourself whether it's a worthwhile use of your time. Let people feel honored when you do say "yes."

When you're setting deadlines for a project, refer to your calendar. Write in a daily chunk of time for the project, and be generous about how long you think it will take using the time you have available. If your calendar is full, try moving the start date of the project up to a point where you do have time.

● ●

Fast Fact

A Luis Harris poll found that Americans are working 20 percent more hours and have 32 percent less leisure time now than in 1973.

● ●

ONE MORE THING

Always leave enough time in your life to do something that makes you happy, satisfied, even joyous. That has more of an effect on economic well-being than any other single factor.

—Paul Hawken

Being able to create and then enjoy free time is an art in itself. But, as you can see from this chapter, it can be done—and done well. You can do it. Just put some of these ideas into action.

As I was writing this chapter, I couldn't help but think of my own life and those of my parents. They came from the old school, where hard work was a necessity and the key to success. An honest buck for an honest day's work. But what about happiness and fun? I would ask. Happiness, they said, is a by-product of hard work. Fun is reserved for kids.

My father has done quite well for himself, a testament to long hours and hard work. For twenty years he worked fourteen hours a day, seven days a week. Did he ever have time for fun? No. He was working.

Because of his success, my father was able to retire at the age of forty-nine. He promised my mother they would do all the things they missed while he was working. They would travel, spend time with the kids and grandchildren.

This never happened. My father soon went back to work, part-time, then full-time, and finally what could be considered overtime. They can't travel much because he is committed to his new business. Today, at fifty-nine, he is working as hard as ever. At the end of the day, he's too tired to do anything but eat dinner and go to sleep.

You can see why my parents had a hard time understanding my need to express myself and to have fun. I have always worked hard, but I also try to enjoy my life. I feel it would be better to learn from their mistakes than to follow in their footsteps. I have learned not to put off living.

3

· · · · ·

LIVE FOR TODAY, PLAN FOR TOMORROW

Getting Your Priorities Straight

When I was on my deathbed, I came to the realization that careers and success and all the things that we worked so hard for all our lives and spend all our time and energy on are really not important.

—*Steve Laury*

You can do anything you want—you just can't do *everything* you want. There simply isn't enough time. That's why you must choose what is most important to you and devote the bulk of your time and energy in that direction. In order to live a balanced, fulfilling, and productive life—or at least to get those other people off your back—you must decide what is most important to you and arrange your time around those things.

For the creative person, however, this is easier said than done.

To the creative person, *everything* can seem like a priority. That's one of the primary struggles—choosing between the good and the best. It's not always obvious which things to put first.

On top of that, you constantly come up with all kinds of new and interesting things to do, creating more work than any mortal could possibly accomplish. Combining flexibility with focus will help you make the most of your eclectic nature. Being a big-picture person, you often have to force yourself to deal with the details of implementing all those ideas. Otherwise you'll just move on to the next thing, leaving project after project unfinished.

You don't have to be "productive" in the obvious sense every waking minute. Indeed, you can't afford to tie yourself to someone else's idea of "productivity." Sometimes the most productive thing you can do today is lie in the grass and watch the clouds go passing by. Recharging your battery is a priority for the creative person—particularly when you habitually light the candle at both ends. Having priorities helps you finish what you start—without burning out and without getting bored.

Prioritize by Sex

Men and women tend to have at least slightly different priorities simply because of gender bias.

	MEN	WOMEN
Health	95%	95%
Rewarding career	71%	51%
Personal relationships	66%	79%
Deeper purpose in life	49%	61%
Spiritual growth	64%	75%
Make a difference in world	55%	64%
Financial success	57%	50%
Raise a family	83%	88%

STUDY BY THE WIRTHLIN REPORT

WHAT ARE YOUR PRIORITIES?

If you are working off the in-box that is fed you, you are probably working on the priorities of others.
—Donald Rumsfeld

Everyone has his or her own agenda. What is a priority to one person doesn't even make the list for another. You can't plan and organize your time if you don't know what *you* are about and what's most important to *you*. Some people have let others tell them what to do for so long, they lose sight of what they want for themselves.

What are your priorities? Only you can answer that question.

If you are unable to rattle off what is most important in your life, you are not alone. One of the most common excuses people use for not deciding what's important is "I'm too busy to slow down and figure out what's important." (This is not a valid excuse, in case you were wondering.) This kind of shortsightedness could be the *reason* you're too busy to slow down in the first place.

How can you manage your life—or even your daily work—by priorities if they're constantly changing? Even if you have a good idea what's most important, it's always good to reevaluate and update your priorities regularly.

Priorities change for many reasons, some of them internal, some external. Artist Susan Rothenberg said in an interview in the early 1970s that having a child was a wake-up call for her career. "I had the very distinct thought that having a child meant I wasn't young anymore. What better demarcation can you have in your life than a baby to make you feel like you can't be a f____ around anymore?"

In the late 1980s, after her daughter left for college, Rothenberg again had a major shift in her career, moving from New York to New Mexico, where she began experimenting with new media. The new surroundings also had a major impact on her imagery.

WHERE YOUR TIME GOES

Time is what we want most but what we use worst.
—William Penn

Some people accomplish nothing, then stop to rest. These people are a whirlwind of activity. Rushing here and there, always busy, always behind. By day's end they realize that they didn't really finish anything, and they didn't even enjoy the ride. Worse still, they feel trapped by the hectic, sometimes empty, life they have created.

Longer hours aren't the answer. If there were more hours in the day, chances are they would fill those with a maddening array of additional meaningless tasks.

Busywork devours more of your time and energy than you are probably willing to admit. The price you pay is even more painful to face. You're exhausted, yet you have very little to show for your efforts. When you consider all the time you've squandered, you realize that life is passing you by and you are going nowhere. Your talents are wasted on tedious, unimportant, trivial things. Your dreams and goals remain far off in the distance. And you let it happen to yourself, because you didn't value your time.

Busyness is often used as a way to avoid intimacy, to sabotage success, or to justify an already sagging self-worth. Procrastination can have the same effect. Both behaviors are rooted in an inability to choose what you want and go for it. Therapy can help. So can sitting down and working out your needs, goals, and priorities (different layers of the same thing).

The first step is to figure out where all that time is wasted.

GETTING YOUR TIME UNDER CONTROL

Knowing when not to work is as important as knowing when to.

—*Harvey MacKay*

Take a close look at your "to do" list. It probably has a lot of unnecessary things on it. Mark them off or hand them off to someone more appropriate. There. You've taken a big step toward catching up already.

There are things that you may never have considered time-wasters that take up your hours, your mental space, and your energy. Consider:

- When you continually choose to do things that provide immediate gratification, you're going to reach a screeching halt someday soon. Life is not a sprint—it's a marathon. All those future-oriented things like setting up appointments and organizing your finances and writing proposals may be a pain to do now, but they're what bring in the work, the fun stuff, the money, in the long run.

- Doing things that are easiest first, things you know you'll succeed at, know you can complete, may seem like a good idea. You like seeing things finished, and this is the quickest way to achieve that satisfaction. However, if you're spending high-energy time on low-energy jobs, you're wasting valuable—and limited—time. Do the easy stuff at the end of the day, when you're a little tired and an easy task is not as daunting as a big project.

- One trivial task usually leads to another. This is a real trap. You never get to the important or long-term jobs because you're so busy tidying up. Working a little bit every day on long-term projects keeps you from facing a leaky roof with a thunderstorm building outside. If you push aside the trivial stuff for a day or two, or even a week, it won't take so long to catch up.

- Doing small, insignificant tasks too well is another trap. Perfectionism in small things can keep you from ever getting to the big stuff. A corporate manager I know spends her weekends polishing her memos, making them neat, tidy, and covering every possible question. Her biggest complaint? Nobody ever seems to read them. Yet she continues to polish, putting her life on hold for work nobody values.

- Most creatives try to do too much. In many cases you might honestly feel that only you can do the job right. If so, allow yourself enough time, or have someone do the groundwork and you do the polish at the end. You won't do the job right if you don't have enough time to do it.

- You underestimate how long it takes to do a given job. Try timing yourself on something simple—a phone call, cleaning the bathroom, sorting the mail. If it doesn't take you twice as long as you thought it would, you're a better person than I am.

- You get sidetracked by emergencies, urgent items that aren't really so urgent. Many people spend so much time "putting out fires" that they never get to the real business at hand. Setting—and sticking to—clear priorities can help you avoid this one.

- You get bored, so you slow down, daydream, doodle, and finally move on to something new. Avoid this by getting up and moving around, brainstorming your project with someone else, or switching to another project for a short time before switching back.

- You get caught up in somebody else's schedule. Athletes learn to avoid this, often the hard way. Mark Allen, for years the top triathlete in the world, won every race except the Ironman, where he lost to Dave Scott over and over again. He finally learned to run his own race, stick to his own rhythms, instead of trying to keep up the killer pace Scott used to wear his competition down. In doing so, Allen beat Scott and went on to more Ironman wins, every one at his own pace.

- Not having a vision for the future can limit your success in the present. It's easier to determine what's important in the short run when you know what you want in the long run. Everything connects.

- Lack of planning leads to poor decisions, doing more than you have to. Have you ever left the house and gotten halfway to work when you remembered something you had forgotten? How much time did you waste turning around, going back, and getting it? How much pay did you lose by being late?

- Too much planning and not enough action can be just as bad as no planning at all. I know a guy who planned out his backyard landscaping in exquisite detail—for years. Once he actually cleared a patch for planting, but he took so long to work out exactly the plants he would put in that weeds grew up in the space and he had to clear it out again.

● ●

Mouse Milking

Doing everything but what you should be doing—that's "milking the mouse." You get a minimum return on maximum effort when you milk a mouse, even a female mouse. It's the ultimate time-waster—but you're busy. You're working hard.

In psychological terms, this is called "avoidance response." Even the most otherwise mundane and tedious things seem like fun when they keep you from doing something you don't want to do. That's when you know you're in trouble. The sense of virtuous justification is soon replaced by guilt and then by stress, because the time you sacrificed to do insignificant tasks could have and should have been used for a more important item.

An acquaintance of mine was commissioned to do several paintings for a new hospital. She was to be well paid and receive great exposure as soon as the paintings were completed. This was important to her career and her livelihood, yet she found herself spending her time on less rewarding things like

- plucking her eyebrows;
- organizing her CDs alphabetically;
- reading the dictionary;
- dusting;
- wandering aimlessly around a department store;
- reorganizing her filing system;
- checking for gray hairs;
- synchronizing her watch with all the clocks in her house;
- ordering lingerie on the Internet.

Now, who's to say these aren't important things to do? She did! She knew what she was supposed to be doing, but she couldn't help herself. When the paintings were due, she hadn't even started. She was so caught up in unimportant tasks, she lost sight of her priorities—and her deadline.

● ●

URGENT VS. IMPORTANT

A man who wants time to read and write lets the grass grow long.

—*Sloan Wilson*

What's the difference between things that are pressing and demand your immediate attention and things that don't necessarily seem urgent but are substantially more important? The urgent tasks make the most noise, crying out for your attention—and they usually get it. They nag at you until you attend to them, but in the overall scheme of things they have very little value. Because they are frantic in nature, you do them first. They are usually false priorities, however—trivial things parading around as all important. Even though they can be quick and easy to do, the reward for doing them is minimal. And because there are so many of them, they crowd out the important things you really should be focusing your time and energy on.

How do you know what is important? Ask yourself, Will doing this matter in a year? Five years? Usually, the things that relate to your core values, dreams, and well-being are important. Because many of these are more long-term in nature, they don't present themselves as pressing. Left unattended, they have a major impact.

To gain control of your time, put first things first. Do the important tasks first—those with the highest payoff—and use whatever time is left to chip away at the "urgent" things. Find ways to do the less important tasks faster. Just remember, it isn't the quantity of things you get done in a day, it's the *quality* of those things.

STICK TO YOUR GUNS

The hardest part about prioritizing is sticking to your guns once you've decided what's most important. Other people will often have conflicting priorities—and you have to learn to deal with that without alienating them or caving in to them. More often, your sense of what's important will change willy-nilly through the day as you jump from project to project. That's why you think things out beforehand. If you have a clear view of what's important and why, you're less likely to be distracted by the events of the day. And you're more likely to recognize it when something really important comes along.

- Let people around you know what your priorities are. Post them on your bulletin board.

- Don't let others pile things on. Just because you *can* do it doesn't mean you should.

- Admit it when you're overbooked. You can do it delicately: "I won't be able to get to that until next week" or "Why don't we discuss this on Tuesday?"

- Make appointments with yourself, and block out time to work on your priorities. A consultant I know gives herself from eight A.M. to ten A.M. to work at home before going into the office. This is her time without interruptions, where she sets priorities and works on her most important projects. Then she's prepared to face the questions and interruptions and conflicting demands of her work group.

- Keep your "to do" list visible. Helen Gurley Brown, founder of *Cosmopolitan* magazine, kept a copy of the magazine on her desk as a reminder of what her priorities were as editor.

- Break down the big tasks into little tasks. The long-term goal is to finish this book. Today's priority is to finish this chapter.

- Balance what you *should* do with what you *want* to do. They're not necessarily different.

- When emergencies arise and you get pulled away from your priorities, get back to them as quickly as possible.

- Cut the dead weight from your "to do" list. Make sure the things you are working on are still needed. I worked on improving a book proposal for weeks in the hopes of landing a book deal. To my surprise, I found out I already had the deal. If I had just asked my agent, I could have saved a lot of work.

- Some minor tasks will solve themselves. Wait three days and see if it is still necessary.

- Don't just start in on whatever's on top of the pile. Do first things first.

- Be flexible. Reevaluate your priorities often.

A Simple Way to Arrange and Rearrange Your Short-Term Priorities

This is a flexible system, so don't be afraid to do this now, even if you're not sure what your priorities are or what they will be next week. Go with what you feel is important today.

(You will need a stack of three-by-five-inch index cards to complete this exercise.)

1. Write down everything you do in a week (one per card).

2. Sort the cards with your weekly tasks on them into three categories:

   - things you must do (parenting, work, commute, cook, clean the cat box)

   - things you want to do (read, watch TV, go out to dinner, walk on the beach)

   - things you don't want to do (scrub the bathtub, play bridge with the Rumfords, clean the catbox)

3. Sort the cards within each stack so that the most important tasks are on top. Eliminate as many cards as you can from the "things you don't want to do" pile and throw them away.

Sort and re-sort as your priorities change and new things are added. The idea is to transfer your daily have-to's into a life of want-to's.

LOOK BEFORE YOU LEAP

Planning is bringing the future into the present so that you can do something about it now.

—Alan Lakein

Just one minute of planning can save thirty minutes of doing things that are a waste of your limited time. Sometimes just the act of planning alone makes a project possible. In the end, you may not follow your plan very closely, but taking the time to plan has many advantages.

When facing an overwhelming or complex endeavor, you have no idea where to start. Planning lets you break it down and find a place to jump in. You can look at the task as a whole (the big picture) or see it as a series of small strides. Either way, you can anticipate potential problems and avert a time-consuming crisis. Looking at the steps required, you can discern what you can (and want to) accomplish yourself and where you'll need a hand. There is no downside to creating a flexible yet functional plan, focusing whatever time, energy, and resources you have at your disposal.

Planning isn't popular with creative people. You would prefer to just jump in and go and through trial and error arrive at the finish line. Unfortunately, along the way you may make several wrong turns, each of which will cost you valuable time, energy, and resources. Even a modest plan can help you avoid wasted motion and minimize your chances of getting sidetracked. Leaving everything to chance usually leads to bad decisions, unrealistic time estimates, missed opportunities, a lack of support from teammates, and a higher cost in terms of time and money.

Planning does not have to be linear, logical, rigid, stuffy, and boring. I wouldn't go so far as to say it's fun, but it can be flexible, pleasurable, and highly functional. As an example, one of my favorite ways to plan a project is to start with a free association exercise (brainstorming combined with Mind Mapping). I use different-colored Post-it notes (some with a single phrase, others with only simple symbols), writing down everything I can think of that needs to be done to complete the job. Then I arrange and rearrange the sequence of events into manageable steps, moving the Post-it notes around a bulletin board. As the project progresses, I adjust the sequence of the steps and augment or eliminate as I go.

Some of the creative person's strongest abilities are used in the planning process, things like imagination, open-mindedness, intuition, big-picture thinking, and visualization. Some forms of planning (like PERT and Gantt charts, blech) involve a degree of number crunching and analytical thinking that may not appeal to you, but they are by no means the only way—or even the best way—to plan a project, a day, a meeting, a meal, a vacation, or anything.

CONVENTIONAL PLANNING TIPS

It is better to have a bad plan than no plan at all.
—*Charles De Gaulle*

The following are some planning tips that encourage the use of your creative strengths while keeping that boring stuff to a minimum.

- Visualize the outcome you are seeking. What will it look like? Is there something similar you can use as a benchmark? What is your overriding objective? What will it do for others? Be able to define your outcome and objective clearly. Stephen Covey says, "The key to creativity is to begin with the end in mind, with a vision and a blueprint of the desired result."

- Gather your tools before you begin planning. Go to the office supply store and buy some fun, colorful supplies to make the planning a little more enjoyable: colored pens, Post-it notes, stickers, index cards, crayons, colored paper, a large board, new software, whatever will make the process more palatable.

- One of the best ways to begin the planning process is to brainstorm ideas. At this point, don't judge your responses. After you have exhausted every possible option, you can begin to eliminate the things that obviously won't work. Then get it on paper!

- Keep it simple. Use visuals, key words, keep it to the point, use terminology that is easy to understand. Don't waste a lot of time spelling things out.

- Be flexible. Don't be afraid to adjust your plan as you go. When you write out your plan, use a format that can be updated easily (pencil, computer, dry wipe board).

- Try different approaches to keep planning interesting (brainstorming, Mind Mapping, charting, storyboarding, in groups or alone).

- Ask these questions at the start of the planning process: What are the biggest challenges I will face? What resources will I need to complete this task? Who can help me? Has anyone already done something comparable? (Can I call them for advice or at least use their plan as a model?) What limitations do I have to work with (time, staff, materials, space, budget)? When is it due? What do I do first?

- "Plan B." Anticipate problems and delays, and try your best to plan for them. Don't let this turn you into a naysayer and squelch your motivation and enthusiasm. Keep a can-do, optimistic outlook, find creative solutions to possible problems—but be realistic as well.

- When a task seems impossible, break things down into the smallest steps possible. You can't clean the whole house before your mother-in-law arrives, but you can 1) clean the bathrooms, 2) sweep, 3) clean off the tables and counters, 4) put fresh linens in the spare bedroom, 5) put flowers on the dining table, and so on. When she gets here, you may have only reached step 3, but you've gotten the most effect for the time you had.

- When listing a task, include an estimate of how long it will take. Use a timeline to lay out when tasks should be completed. This may sound a bit too corporate for your tastes, but it's visual in a way that you're likely to relate to better than a calendar. You can see what comes first, when, and you can tell right away when you're falling behind. You can even have some fun making it colorful or artful as you think about what goes where.

- Set a firm but realistic deadline. Many creative people are most effective, inspired, and energized when facing a deadline.

- Keep in mind that things take twice as long as you anticipate. Actually, my editor says it's three times as long and I'm just overoptimistic. Pad your plan to allow for this—as well as all the stuff you didn't think of.

- Leave time in your plan for conceptualizing.

- When making your plan, allow time to recharge between tasks, to take a break. Don't schedule (and count on being able to work) every waking minute. If you run your own business, plan one day out of every five (eight hours out of every forty) to handle business maintenance stuff like paperwork, banking, mail, filing, learning new skills, handling personnel issues, networking, client meetings, and so on.

- Pace yourself (and your team) as you go. One of the biggest problems is spending too much time on one area in the early stages and then having to rush on the tasks toward the end.

- Establish rewards for your minor victories. If you complete a certain portion of your plan by this date, you get a prize. (This doesn't work if you give yourself the prize anyway.)

- If you are working with others, organize your team around the project and find the talent to match the task.

- Some things have to be done in a sequential order. Plan for that.

- Ask yourself why you are doing each task in your plan. This will help you discard needless work.

● ●

Be Prepared

You will never be able to anticipate everything that could go wrong or that has to be done. Try this exercise. You are planning a group picnic. List all the things you will need to make it go smoothly.

(Did you remember to arrange for invitations, directions, transportation, toilet facilities, activities or games, table coverings, ice, shade, bug spray, utensils (including a corkscrew and bottle opener), and cleanup? What am I forgetting?

● ●

QUESTION

In order to succeed, you must know what you are doing, like what you are doing, and believe in what you are doing.

—*Will Rogers*

Question everything. It's a basic way to get that brain working. See how many questions you can come up with without straying off the point. Then find answers (that's the hard part)—and you've got the basis for a solid plan.

● Ask *what if* questions. (What if I did this? What if I tried that?)

● What is the objective? What am I trying to create?

● What's unique about it?

● What do I already have? What's missing? (Now you know the gap between the vision and the reality.)

● How will I know when I'm getting off track?

● How can I streamline?

● What should I replace?

● Is there a better way to do it?

● How can I simplify?

● What can I improve? What can I do better?

● What's the next step?
(Don't forget the who, what, where, why, when, how, and how much questions.)

BRAINSTORMING/FREE FLOW

The only true happiness comes from squandering ourselves for a purpose.

—John Mason Brown

This is the best first step after you take on a project that requires planning. The idea in the initial planning stage is to come up with as many choices as possible. Go wild. It is a total brain dump at this stage. It's about quantity, not quality. Throw all your ideas at the wall and see what sticks. It's often best to do this with at least one other person. Interaction creates a synergy that can be incredibly creative, not to mention fun.

Then throw out the bad ideas—but don't be too quick about it. Just because it's never been done before doesn't mean you can't do it.

1. State the project clearly.

2. Generate as many ways to attack the project as possible. (Don't evaluate their validity at this point.)

3. When the smoke clears, discuss, evaluate, and eliminate.

4. Sift and sort and decide the order and sequence of what's left.

MIND MAPPING

I would rather live at a heightened level than live the dull, commonplace life of the average person.

—Janice Rule

Mind Mapping was developed by Tony Buzan as a powerful tool to engage your right brain in the planning and note-taking process. It's a fast (and effective) way to formulate plans using word and idea association. You rely on key words, colors, and graphics to form a nonlinear action plan. When you are done, you have a drawing that looks like a person standing with legs apart and arms outstretched, with words growing out of each appendage.

Rather than demanding a linear, sequential list as you would in a traditional outline or "to do" list, Mind Mapping encourages you to put your ideas and information into a visual, interconnected form that enhances creativity and flexibility. It works extremely well on everything from planning a project to planning your week.

Begin by putting a broad idea or specific project in a circle in the center of the page. As related ideas come to you, draw a line outward from the core idea. Your ideas extend out like spokes from the hub on a wheel. You layer them with subpoints or subcircles.

This works so well with creative people because it is both visual and interconnected. By seeing your thoughts in written form, you get an overview that allows you easily to understand and link tasks together. Because this process uses more of the creative side of your brain than a traditional outline or "to do" list, you spend less time and energy trying to sequentially list things in a particular order. You get things on paper faster and more freely without any left-brain interference.

HOW TO MIND MAP A "TO DO" LIST

Holding a clean piece of paper horizontally (more room to write), begin with the biggest challenge or project for the day in the middle of the page and circle it. Now write down whatever ideas, solutions, and related tasks come to mind. Let ideas flow from your head to your hand without any censorship— just write them down as quickly as possible (use key words or symbols in their own bubbles) and then watch the form take shape. Connect related tasks and ideas from the central idea with lines.

You can add to it at any time, which saves you from having to keep making new "to do" lists. You can see the results of your efforts over the week as you cross off completed items. It's also quick—in ten minutes you should have a workable week-long schedule, or project overview, or problem work-around. You can use Mind Mapping for almost any kind of planning.

Keep your old Mind Maps—they'll become works of art as you use them. Keep adding to them as ideas come to you. Put them up on the wall.

OTHER WAYS

The creative person can come up with all kinds of great ideas but is all over the place when it comes to putting them into practical, usable form so that a plan of action can be developed. Here are several techniques to form flexible plans of action that work with the creative person's natural gifts. These ideas can help you break your traditional patterns of thinking, move you beyond your narrow perspective and out of your comfort zone to aid you in your creative planning.

INDEX CARDS. Write your plan on index cards and post them on corkboard, pin them to the wall, rubber-band them in sequence, keep them in a recipe box holder with divider tabs. This works particularly well with complex projects that involve groups of people or many interrelated steps. It helps you keep everything straight—and keeps you from losing somebody or leaving out an important part of the job. It's also flexible—if an item becomes irrelevant or a group member takes maternity leave, you can toss the card or transfer their job onto somebody else's card (not yours).

POST-IT NOTES. Arrange Post-it notes with tasks on a board and move them around as the plan develops and changes. This is one of the most flexible forms of planning and works best in the original stages, when parameters are still being defined. Make your idea board visual and leave it out in the open where you can see it and add to it daily. Nobody says planning has to be done all at one sitting.

SLEEP ON IT. Let your subconscious solve your planning problems while you sleep. Before going to bed, think hard about the project and the problems associated with it (without creating a case of insomnia). The answers are usually waiting for you in the morning. If you have trouble remembering your dreams, the next best thing is meditation and visualization to tap into your subconscious mind, where a lot of the best ideas reside. (Use your conscious mind to implement the planning.)

WHOLE-BRAIN PLANNING. Ideas come from the right side of your brain, but the left brain puts them into a logical sequence. To tap into both sides of the brain, turn your paper on its side and fold it in half. Use the left side of the page to outline your plan and the right side to sketch or Mind Map it.

SWITCH HITTER. Another whole-brain approach is to plan and engage both sides of your brain by formulating a plan first with your writing hand, and then with your other hand. These should end up being quite different. Use the best of both lists.

WHAT IF. What if a famous, successful, innovative person (whom you admire and know something about) were to help you plan? What do you think he or she would suggest? Think as this person would think.

PLAY. Loosen up, let go, and play to come up with the most innovative plans. Steven Spielberg's office is filled with video games and pinball machines. Why not keep some fun stuff around to help you get in touch with your creativity—toys like Lego, Silly Putty, or even a rubber chicken? Play facilitates the free flow of ideas and thoughts.

SENSORY PERCEPTION. How will it feel, smell, look, sound, and taste when completed? The more tangible your goal, the better you can visualize it.

DOODLE. This is a wonderful technique for planning. Don't worry about the artistic integrity of your drawing. It isn't about the result of your doodle per se. The magic is in the process.

STOP AND DO SOMETHING ELSE. Read, listen to music, garden, go for a drive, smoke a cigar (my personal favorite)—whatever relaxes you and disengages your logic brain for a while. Einstein played the violin for a diversion. The environment you do your planning in can affect the results of those efforts. Retreat to a quiet, idea-friendly, peaceful place to do your planning. Go for a walk and "think on your feet."

SOFTWARE. There are several excellent software programs that can turn your ideas into outline form and complete workable plans. These electronic outlining programs are also handy to use for scheduling. If you are on a network, people can view and download updated versions of the plan, add to it, report on their progress and any problems they may be encountering. One program in particular, IdeaFisher, asks a series of questions to prompt you in the creative planning process.

ELIMINATE NEGATIVE THINKING. Killer phrases like "We've tried that before and it didn't work" or "It will never work" are counterproductive. Someone once said, "It is the unquestioning acceptance of the already existing that keeps people from being creative." Don't do this to yourself—and don't let others do it to you, either.

ONGOING PLANNING. If possible, keep your plans with you so that when you have an insight, you can add it in. I keep ongoing projects in my planner so that I can doodle, debate, and design on the road.

CREATE A PICTURE BOOK. This works particularly well for those who don't feel comfortable with words. Draw or find pictures (all my magazines are cut to bits) to represent what you need done and the steps you will take to do it. While this can be time-consuming (unless you're a rapid sketch artist), the time spent looking for or creating pictures to represent the process is also being spent thinking about the plan. Not a waste at all.

ENCOURAGE INPUT EARLY. Architect Rob Quigley is in charge of designing a new central library for the city of San Diego. Early in the planning stages, he sought input from the people who will use it—the citizens of San Diego. He called a meeting, and after handing everyone an index card, he asked that they let their imaginations soar and write a three-word message to him about their vision for what this new library should be. He then posted the cards on the wall. The responses ranged from "Keep it quiet" (good idea) to "Give it warmth" to "Friendly, comfortable, local." Afterward Quigley commented, "This process will be immensely helpful in going in the right direction so we don't burn up your money going in the wrong direction." Amen.

STORYBOARDING. I believe this was first used at Disney. It's a good way to get a group or team involved, encourage input, and weed out the best from the rest. (It is also a very quick way to plan, saving a great deal of time.)

1. Give everyone a felt-tip marker and several five-by-eight-inch index cards.

2. Pose the problem, project, or outcome you are planning for. Write it on a board where everyone can see it.

3. Ask for ideas, with the only caveat being that responses must be brief (one to four words per card) and only one idea per card.

4. Give them a time limit, collect the cards, and post them on the wall.

5. Group the cards into categories and discard the duplicates.

6. Create category headings and, with input from the group, arrange the ideas into a workable plan.

7. Assign responsibilities.

8. Transfer the plan to paper (or take a picture of it) and distribute copies to everyone to implement.

There are many ways to plan—but then, there are many things to plan for and many situations where planning is important. Whether you're working alone or with others, on a job or running a household, planning can help you manage your time, minimize your distractions, handle crises as they occur, and maximize your success. Go for it!

4
• • • • •

TUNE IN, TURN ON

How to Focus on More Than One Thing at a Time

> *I arise each morning torn between a desire to save the world and a desire to savor the world. That makes it hard to plan the day.*
>
> —E. B. White

The creative person's brain is a lot like a CD changer set on "shuffle play." It can focus in short bursts (the length of a song), but at the same time it needs variety, so it shifts randomly from CD to CD until all the songs have been played. Being a creative, divergent thinker can be both a blessing and a curse—it all depends on how many songs you've got in your stack.

The creative person embraces and even thrives on chaos that would overwhelm a mere mortal. For the creative person, handling many projects at once is not so much natural as it is necessary. There are a number of reasons for this:

● A need for immediate gratification.

● A craving for new challenges.

● The ability to find fascination in nearly everything.

● Extreme distractability.

● A resistance to constriction in any area of life.

● Boundless energy.

● Imagination, the ability to create new things.

● Difficulty in making decisions or setting limits.

Before Phil Collins had a successful solo career, he was "only" the frontman and drummer for Genesis. He felt a bit stifled creatively and wanted to experiment with other forms of music. So he joined a band called Brand X, where he could perform more improvisational music.

"Brand X was where I went to have fun," Collins said. "An analogy would be that it was a place I could go and take off all of my clothes and live, to do things I couldn't do with Genesis."

JUGGLING WORKS

I . . . have to constantly juggle being a writer with being a wife and mother. It's a matter of putting two different things first, simultaneously.

—Madeleine L'Engle

When you're able to effectively juggle several things at once, yet still concentrate on one at a time when you have to, you can be extremely efficient with your time. If you are waiting on something—a callback, more information, a meeting, somebody's approval—to continue with a project, you can change gears and work on another project in the interim. The reason this works is that although you have shifted gears, *you're still moving forward.*

Use the same technique for those times when you are bored, burned out, or blocked with a particular project. Downshift to something less taxing or simply something different. As long as you stay in gear, as long as you keep moving, you're accomplishing something—and you're not losing that precious creative momentum.

Being a nonlinear thinker has other advantages. You can jump in wherever you feel comfortable. You don't have to start at the beginning and work in a sequential manner. You can work in much the same way film directors do, shooting scenes out of order to use resources more effectively. Being able to see the big picture helps you match tasks to your mood and energy levels.

To keep your mind active, use multitasking (fancy word for juggling) for simple, otherwise boring things. Leonardo da Vinci took notes with one hand while drawing with the other. If you don't have enough projects to keep you moving forward, look for new things to try, new and diverse skills to learn. Put some effort into gaining experience. Limited experience can mean a limited life, creative stagnation, and ultimate frustration.

This does not mean you should clutter up your life with meaningless things to do. It simply means action breeds energy, both mental and physical. Once you stop (exercising, thinking, or creating), it's much harder to start again. So keep moving, keep the balls in the air.

Michael Crichton is a master juggler—a physician-turned-computer-game-designer-turned-nonfiction-author-turned-novelist-turned-screenwriter-turned-director-turned-producer He is known for his intellectual curiosity, which has taken him in a number of different directions. As a result, he's kept moving forward, creating an amazingly diverse body of work, which includes *Jurassic Park, Disclosure, Rising Sun,* and *ER.* Juggling can work!

WHEN JUGGLING DOESN'T WORK

We're always doing something, talking, reading, listening to the radio, planning what's next. The mind is kept naggingly busy on some easy, unimportant external thing all day.

—Brenda Veland

There are more advantages than disadvantages to being a proficient juggler, but there are some pitfalls. These include the following:

- Buzzing around wasting energy on a number of unimportant things that eat up your time. Busywork does provide you with the satisfaction of completing minor tasks, but it gets in the way of real accomplishment.

- Switching gears is the ideal way to give yourself a much needed break from time to time. Problems arise when that little break turns into a major distraction and you have a hard time getting back to the project at hand.

- I am sure you have heard the expression "a man of many talents, all of them minor." That's the risk you run if you find yourself frequently flitting from job to job, always searching for something new, always thinking the grass is greener elsewhere. Juggling means working both sides of the room, not leaving the house altogether.

- Lack of follow-through is distressing to us and others. No matter how creative you are or how many projects you can juggle, if you never finish anything, you're going nowhere.

- If you try juggling too many things at once, you'll know it. You start losing things, missing deadlines, leaving a lot of loose ends. You stop being creative and interesting and end up pressured, hurried, and grouchy.

- Others who know you are a master juggler have a tendency to keep throwing things at you. Make sure you're juggling *your* stuff, not somebody else's.

HOW TO JUGGLE

What are your limitations? What is your weekly work capacity? How long can you go without a break? How many things can you comfortably juggle at one time? Knowing your limitations will help you avoid a meltdown later.

- Admit that there's a limit to how much you can juggle. Singer/songwriter Michael Franks admits, "I've been trying to write a book, between tours, recording, and a Broadway project about Gauguin, and believe me, it's not easy."

- When things get out of hand and you have too much on your plate, push everything aside and take stock. Establish a hierarchy of what's most important and should be done first and what can wait. It's good to take the time to get that overview perspective every now and then anyhow. It helps you avoid getting caught up in the swirl and losing direction—and it helps you avoid maxing out your time/energy resources.

- When you are past your limit and can't take on anything else, say "no"—not just to others, but to yourself. And be confident about saying it.

- Stay away from boring and repetitive work. Use your assets. Don't enter into projects that will take an eternity or deals that reward you only at the end.

- Maintain a balance between structure and freedom. Some order will help you keep more balls in the air, without stifling your creativity.

- Match the task to your energy level.

- Pay attention to deadlines. Keep a written record of all the things you are juggling and when they are due. This could be in the form of a project board on the wall, in your planner or calendar, a notebook, or just where you position your piles (those closest to my desk are the most urgent).

- Know your attention span and plan around it. If you block out four hours to work on one project, but you can focus for a maximum of only one hour, it might be better to work on four different projects for one hour each.

- Don't force yourself to work on a project until you are bored or burned out. On the other hand, when you are "in the zone" and completely focused on the task at hand, where everything you do is magic, keep going as long as you can.

- Change creative gears every once in a while. Are you a writer? Try painting. Celebrity artists include Anthony

Quinn, Tony Bennett, Phyllis Diller. Writers-turned-musicians include Amy Tan, Dave Barry, and Stephen King. Right-brain/left-brain switch-offs keep you moving forward.

- When you switch from one project to the next, leave off at an easy point to pick up again. It helps to make a note or some indication of where you were and where you were going so you don't waste time backtracking when you switch back.

As a drummer, I know that the guys in the band are counting on me to provide a steady beat. On most tunes, that's my role. But sometimes when I'm sitting back there playing the same beat over and over, I just have to do something to break up the monotony. Within the context of the song, I can add a "fill" or a "roll" and still maintain the groove of the music. But you have to pick your spots. You can't be all over the place (unless you're Keith Moon). It would ruin the song and upset the other band members.

Drummers—and all creative people, for that matter—have to have some degree of discipline when it comes to indulging their impulses to jump around. Combining focus with some flexibility can make for a happy compromise everyone can live with.

● ●

One of Us

PAUL PETERSEN, ILLUSTRATOR

How do you fit the juggling of tasks into your work style?

I like to have several tasks going on at the same time in my work space. That way, when I am tempted to take a break, I can switch tasks instead and it sort of *seems* like a break. I am also proficient at multitasking. For instance, when I am too busy to stop and exercise, I'll jog, walk, or ride my bike to the store or post office instead. That way I can run my errands and get some exercise at the same time.

When faced with a deadline, how do you focus so you finish on time?

In the past, I've set it up so that I had to finish my work before I could use the space for something non-work related. For example, I used to use my bed next to my drawing table as a temporary table for my art materials. I couldn't go to sleep until I could clear off the bed, and I didn't want to clear off the bed until I finished the project.

I'm sure that resulted in a few sleepless nights. Is there anything else you do to help you focus?

When I'm drawing or on a deadline, I screen my calls so I'm not interrupted. I also like to listen to the radio when I work. It reduces the boredom, and I work more efficiently when my mind is alert and receptive. Plus, I'm able to work longer with less tedium.

● ●

DRIVEN TO DISTRACTION (FOCUSING)

The main thing is to keep the main thing the main thing.

—*Stephen Covey*

It's amazing how quickly and efficiently you can get things done when you're focused. This can be with a wide-angle lens or a zoom lens; as long as you narrow your field of vision, you can harness and direct your energy and efforts toward meaningful accomplishments.

Don't think I'm talking about single-mindedness or inflexibility. You can be crazy and creative yet still able to focus when it counts on what counts most. Just a small amount of concentrated effort toward your goals will pay off. Author and motivator Zig Ziglar said it best: "You can't make it as a wandering generality, you have to be a meaningful specific."

A lack of focus can be an asset, to a point. Daydreaming, hyperactivity, divergent thinking—all are functions of lack of focus. Unfortunately so are impulsiveness, inconsistency, poverty, and low self-esteem.

WHY FOCUS?

Concentration is the secret of strength.
—Ralph Waldo Emerson

Like focusing the sun's energy through a magnifying glass, your creativity is more powerful when the beam is narrow and steady. If you can focus, you can do almost anything. It is perhaps the single biggest reason for success and the number one cause of failure.

Without focus, life is hard. You do too many meaningless things in a scattered, fragmented approach to your career, your life. A little of this, a little of that, a lot of nothing, really. Creative people create. Focus on that.

As someone who was once "all over the place," I have come to realize the power of focusing. By concentrating and consolidating my efforts, I have seen a big surge forward in my business, writing career, and even in my golf game. With fewer things going on, it's easier to concentrate on what *is* going on.

If you do just a little each day in the key areas of your life, it starts to add up. Over the course of a year, you start to see some real progress. (In addition, there is nothing like the pleasure and satisfaction of finishing things.) Leaving tasks unfinished and dreams unrealized is sad and depressing. You let others down—you let yourself down. I have seen it happen all too often, and I vowed not to let it happen to me.

DEALING WITH DISTRACTIONS

I enjoy writing in the desert. There are no distractions such as telephones, theaters, opera houses, and gardens.

—Agatha Christie

What is your biggest distraction? What are you going to do about it?

I'm very easily distracted in the bookstore. I tend to forget what I went in for, spend half a day looking through the stacks, chatting with people, getting caught up in the magazine aisle—and wander out, my book budget spent, my original project stalled out.

When it comes to distractions, you're likely to be your own worst enemy. But there are plenty of others who will add confusion and chaos to your day. The boss who needs this *right now* (and will later need the project you set aside for his urgent problem *right now*). The co-worker who was supposed to have the information for project A to you last week and finally gets it to you just when you're scheduled to start project B. The friend who's having a crisis and needs you this minute. The spouse who refuses to let you reschedule your anniversary.

The world is full of people who want to mess with your time. Most of them you can't control, so you smile—or yell—and handle it. The best way to handle outside distractions is to manage the ones you put in your own path.

- If you're constantly checking the traffic out your window, move your desk or shut the blinds.

- I had my wife take the TV remote with her to work, because I just couldn't leave it alone during the day.

- I holed up in a hotel for a few days to finish this book. My wife wanted to come with me and was miffed when I explained she was too distracting. But if you saw her, you'd understand.

- The phone and the mail are big distractions for me. I used to stop and chat, losing track of where I was and where I was going. I'd stop everything when the mail came and sort through it, losing my concentration on the project at hand. Anything new is better than what I'm doing now, right? Wrong. Now I stick the mail in a bin to work on at low-energy times, and I put on the answering machine during working hours.

- You hate to be the bad guy, and you want to help others. That's not so bad. Just keep your office door closed when you need to concentrate. Use a "Do Not Disturb" sign. A lock is good. A deadbolt, maybe chains. A sign tattooed on your forehead that says "When I'm done with my work, I'll be glad to help you with yours."

- Pick your times to be available. "Can we do this at three?" "I'm available at three, how about you?" "Great! Let's talk about this at lunch!" If you really want to be nice, buy lunch.

- Avoid jobs where you're paid to get interrupted, like customer service. The customers will love you; your boss won't.

- All distractions aren't bad. As long as you're getting your work done when you need it done, pleasant distractions (not irritating ones) keep your brain alive.

- Yes, you *can* be tough. In the middle of something important, getting jerked out of your trance can make you angry, frustrated, ruin your work. If you yell then, it's too late to do you any good. It's better to demand the privacy, the uninterrupted time you need now—and be pleasant later.

- If you want to lead the orchestra, you must turn your back to the crowd. You're not going to make everybody happy. Live with it.

- Take your work elsewhere, so you're not readily available.

- Shorten outside interruptions by asking people to get to the point. "I only have a minute. You wanted . . . ?"

- If you're interrupted by an unrelated flash of brilliance, write it down, then get back to work on the project at hand.

- Have all the supplies you need before beginning and arrange your work space so everything you need is in reach. If you have to get up to go to the printer or get a file or supplies, you're opening yourself up to distractions.

- Use something to remind you to focus. Alarm watch. Timer. Trinket. Sign.

- Control the noise in your work space (trucks, air conditioner, phone, fax, kids, radio, TV). Some thrive with certain kinds of noise, but nobody thrives with every kind. Create a quiet zone—unless you're one of those distracted by silence.

- Turn off the phone and doorbell ringers; you won't be tempted to pick up the phone or answer the door if you can't hear them.

- Come in early, stay late (one or the other—not both).

- One distraction leads to another. It's easier to go cold turkey than pretend you can handle just this one.

- If you work at home, make your office off-limits during business hours.

EMERGENCIES

When it hits the fan, don't fight it. After all, one of your strengths is your flexibility. Don't spaz. Put that adrenaline to good use. Go back to your project and finish it when you've dealt with the crisis. Forget about it until then.

Many kinds of crises can conflict with your work, your creative time, your hard-won private time. Kids get sick, a new project suddenly rears its ugly head, deadlines get moved up, you lose something, the computer breaks down, the car flakes out on you, the roads are washed out, and the materials you need won't reach you until doomsday.

The best way to deal with emergencies is to prevent them wherever possible. Anticipate, watch for signals. Don't expect the worst, but be prepared.

- Don't freak. Keep your cool and make plans to catch up later.

- Is it really an emergency? Is it *your* emergency? Someone else's deal?

- Bend, don't break.

- Don't go flying off half-cocked. Think about the best way to deal with the situation. Use that creative brain to come up with solutions. *Then* act.

- Find appropriate help.

DISCIPLINE

Nothing determines who we will become as much as those things we choose to ignore.

—Sandor McNab

Vincent van Gogh would beat himself with a stick if he did not concentrate on his work. He also cut off his earlobe, but that's another story. Jack London worked eighteen-hour days and wrote fifty books in sixteen years; then, at age forty, he killed himself. These are not good examples to follow.

In learning to focus, be realistic. Work with your faults as well as your (hoped-for) virtues. Work around your limitations. Let yourself have fun. Pay attention to your daydreams—they can come in very handy in the real world. Be careful that your self-imposed limits don't stifle creativity.

Some experts believe the maximum time people can really focus today is five minutes. Most say it's no more than ninety minutes. Your own ability to focus will depend on how interested you are. In general, short bursts of activity, followed by a change of pace or change of project, are most effective.

I'm a disciplined writer. I write every day, want to or not. Others wait for their muse to show up and work furiously when it does. I'm always afraid my muse won't show up on time. So I've developed a few strategies to help me focus, even when the surf is calling—because a deadline is a deadline, and my reputation means a lot to me.

- Binge. Lock yourself away when faced with a crisis or deadline. No distractions, no dinner parties, no movies, no visitors. Emerge squinting and very apologetic, but finished. The upside of this one is bingeing on the fun stuff when the job is done. The downside is burnout.

- Focus on gain, not pain. Imagine how it will feel to finish instead of letting your psyche be crushed by the weight of the work to be done. It's better to think about the glory of a new baby in your arms than to worry about the delivery.

- Focus on the positive. Knock those negative thoughts out of your head before they get a chance to take hold and drag you down. Positive thinking is a great energy source. This is Pollyanna talking.

- Take off your watch and lose yourself in a project. Don't let time impinge on your creative process. You can make your apologies when you come up for air.

- Do a brain dump. Don't stop to evaluate, edit, or critique. This lets your subconscious get into the picture, and frequently you'll find the focus you need—it will leap out at you from your own words. Do the polishing, fine-tuning, later.

- Always start work at a set time, so focusing in on your job becomes second nature.

- Find a quiet space to work in. Even more important, find quiet in your head.

- Play classical music. Largo movements from classical composers have a slower cadence than the average heartbeat, which improves concentration.

- A cool breeze, an open window, bright light, aromatherapy—all can trigger your ability to buckle down to the task at hand.

- Eat! You can't focus on an empty stomach, unless you're focusing on what to have for dinner.

- Pretend you're going on a vacation. It's amazing how much you can get done with a big reward waiting. Then take that vacation!

● ●

One of Us

MICHAEL E. ARTH, ARCHITECT, ARTIST, WRITER

What is your best timesaving tip?

My biggest time-saver is being truly interested in what I'm doing. If I don't have that, then everything in life is a distraction. If I am truly interested in a project, all those external things that vie for my attention aren't a distraction. Motivation for me comes when I am totally interested in what I'm doing.

How do you juggle so many things at once?

I'm very project oriented. I get almost completely involved in one project. I'll start thinking about another project usually while I am nearing the end of the one I'm working on. I'll stick to one thing, finish it, then move on to the next one. There is a great sense of satisfaction that comes with finishing what you start—which for me only lasts about four minutes, then I'm on to the next project.

It sounds like you are able to combine creativity with commitment to achieve your goals. Is that the best approach when it comes to focus?

The difference between the fully realized plodder and a fully realized creative person is this: Plodders will set a destination on the horizon for their little skiff on the ocean of life and through sheer determination will get there no matter what. A creative person will sometimes set a destination on the horizon, be driven by curiosity, or be floating adrift.

However, if the creative person has a goal, that person will be flexible enough to change course in order to make new footprints on an undiscovered island.

Creativity by itself isn't enough. Creativity and determination together allow creativity to be fully realized. It's important to have childlike and playful qualities, but also a high degree of responsibility and discipline.

● ●

5

● ● ● ● ●

TIMING IS EVERYTHING

*Being in the Right Place at the Right Time
with the Right Stuff*

*I'm always interested in the right things at the
wrong time.*

—Andy Warhol

We seem to have developed a herd mentality in this country. Everyone wants to do the same things at the same time. Like lambs to slaughter, we fight rush-hour traffic each day, cash our paychecks on Friday afternoon, and consistently wait for a table for two as we join the rest of the world for a noon lunch. Doing things at off-peak hours saves a lot of time (and stress).

Do things when others don't. It's a simple yet effective time management concept, and one that is rarely adhered to (to judge by increasing rush-hour traffic). What day, and what time of the day, you do something can have an impact on how long it will take. To save time, plan your schedule to avoid peak times. When you go against the flow, you can avoid maddeningly long lines, needless delays, and over-crowding. Come into work early or late and avoid the traffic (except in Los Angeles, where there is *always* traffic), go to lunch before noon or after two P.M., and avoid the post office on April 14—see, no problem.

The following are the best ways to avoid the maddening crowds:

● The least busy days at the automated teller machine are Tuesday, Thursday, and Sunday.

- The best time to get a haircut and avoid the wait (assuming you don't have an appointment) is one to four P.M., Monday through Wednesday. (You get a better cut, too, because the hairstylists are less harried.)
- To avoid long checkout lines and crowded parking lots, do your grocery shopping on Tuesday or Wednesday evening. (The shelves are usually well stocked, too.) Any day after nine P.M. also works.
- The best time to see a doctor is first thing in the morning or be the first patient after lunch (you usually don't have to wait).
- The best time of year to go to Disney World? Fall is the least crowded. The best weather is January–February.
- According to a Day-Timers, Inc., study, 58 percent of respondents take care of their most urgent business first thing in the morning. Most people are most alert in late morning and midevening.

THE WORST OF TIMES

Trust yourself. Your perceptions are often far more accurate than you are willing to believe.
—Claudia Black

Just as there is a best time to do things, there is also a worst:
- The worst time to get a haircut is just before Mother's Day, Easter, and back-to-school time.
- The worst times to do your grocery shopping are weekend mornings.
- The worst time to go to the post office is noon to two P.M.
- The worst time to go to the bank is Friday (no kidding, huh?).

- The worst time to buy shoes is first thing in the morning, according to shoe designer Kenneth Cole. To get the best fit, wait until the late afternoon or early evening, when your foot is slightly swollen. How does this relate to time management? If you've ever tried to return a slightly used pair of shoes that doesn't fit, you'll know it's not easy—and very time-consuming.

TIMING TIPS

If you are having difficulties with a book, try the element of surprise: attack it at an hour when it isn't expecting it.

—H. G. Wells

In addition to beating the crowds, doing the right thing at the right time can increase your efficiency. For instance, fitness expert Covert Bailey says the best time to work out is whenever you'll do it regularly, adding that mornings are still the best. Statistics bear that out. People who exercise in the afternoon or evening have the highest dropout rate. With a whole day to think about it, it's easier to create excuses for not working out.

- Don't schedule creative work for times when you know there will be interruptions. Of course, you can't always predict when your elusive muse will show up, and sometimes it hits when you least expect it. Still, trying to do focused work through constant interruptions is next to impossible.

- An insurance company study indicates that most accidents happen between one and three P.M. and between two and four A.M. These are times when most people experience an energy low. Don't plan delicate, taxing, or important work at these times, and avoid driving then if possible.

- It is not a good idea to make potentially life-changing decisions when you are feeling depressed, hopeless, or overly optimistic. It skews your perspective. When you have time to think about it with a clear head, you may find you have created unrealistic deadlines and made more work for yourself.

- Go with the flow. But, as odd as this sounds, spontaneity requires planning and preparation. Author Denis Waitley says, "Your success is not a matter of being in the right place at the right time nearly as much as it is a matter of taking the time to determine what the right place and time ought to be."

- Strike while the iron is hot. If you walk into your office or studio and feel a sudden surge of creativity, don't wait until you have time: use it *now*. There may never be a time when you are clicking as you are right then. Other things can wait.

- The myth about the early bird always getting the worm is based on a false premise. Sometimes the worm isn't worth getting. Rushing to be the first person somewhere, only to have to wait, isn't effective time management. Being the first to do something can mean you are a leader—and that is a good thing. Other times it's best to wait until you are better prepared. Actress Gwyneth Paltrow *(Emma, Seven)* turned down several lead roles early in her career. She didn't feel she was ready at that point. It turned out to be the right thing to do.

- I try to remain as flexible as I can. Occasionally there are days when something comes up (usually when a swell hits) that I want to take advantage of. So I will rearrange my schedule to take that day off and make it up later. (There is no way to predict when the waves will come up, so . . .) Some of the most memorable days of my life have come on those spontaneous days off. Be flexible, in the moment—but be responsible at the same time. If I take off Friday, I'll make it up on Sunday. The key is, I *do* make it up.

- I like working weekends and having weekdays free. The things I want to do on my off days are far less crowded on a Monday than on a Sunday. Plus, like many creative people, I like being different! As John Coltrane once said, "If you are playing jazz, you have to play what comes out at any given moment."

- There are days when you just aren't running on all cylinders. This may be a good time to shut off the engine, put the car in neutral, and coast. (Use this as a day to diddle.) Shift to a lower gear and drive at half speed. Maybe you could use this downtime to take care of little things you have been putting off, things that you can easily complete—rack up a few victories to improve your mood or take care of things that have been nagging at you.

- Jump into something at a point that feels right to you. Many times things will organize themselves; you just need to get started. If you are waiting for inspiration, do some part of the project that doesn't require it. I know a travel writer who starts her stories with the "How to Get There" section. She says it gets her started thinking about where she went and who she saw and what fun she had—and the story itself just spills out.

- Maybe it wasn't meant to be. If you took on something you really can't or don't want to do, admit it. Let it go.

- I picked up a great tip from an interior designer friend who said that she saves her easiest tasks for the end of each day. That way she has a couple of small successes to end each day on a positive note.

WHAT IS YOUR PRIME TIME?

I don't believe in an afterlife. I don't even believe in this life. . . . If there is an afterlife, I guess I'd use it to return phone calls.

—Fran Lebowitz

I can work creatively from about nine A.M. to noon. If I'm on a tight deadline, I can squeeze out another couple of hours. After that, all that comes out is drivel. I'll get my second wind after dinner and go from eight P.M. until two A.M. When I pay attention to my inner clock, I can get a lot more quality creative work done during the day.

Are you a morning person or a night owl? Everyone is different. Some start slow, others start out the day with a bang. Hemingway began writing at first light and would go until late morning. Henry Miller preferred the hours between nine A.M. and one P.M. Anthony Burgess wrote in the afternoon (because he claimed his unconscious mind could better assert itself), and William Faulkner could write only when it rained. Go figure!

One of the keys to time management is *Don't waste your peak hours.* Don't waste your prime time on after-hours-type tasks. You get a much higher return on your investment of time if you schedule your most important work during your peak hours. So protect it, guard it, use it wisely!

Most people use their mornings for clerical work and meetings. By the time they get to their creative or important work, they are too tired or have acquired more things to do along the way. They either don't get around to it, rush it, or are not mentally alert enough to do it well.

Many successfully creative people don't take calls in the morning and set their meetings for the afternoon. Use the first two hours of the day to do your most difficult, creative, important work. Earmark whatever time your energy and enthusiasm are at their highest. Block it out on your calendar and don't waste it on anything else.

Use your off-peak times for mundane or unpleasant tasks, calls, meetings. Do less taxing jobs before going to bed. Don't make tough decisions when you're tired.

Experiment with doing things at different times and see if it doesn't make a difference in both the quantity and quality of work you can get done.

WORK WITH IT

Daylight savings time blossoms once more and is welcomed heartily by insomniacs who now have less night to be up all of.

—*Fran Lebowitz*

Creative people are nonconformists (but then, you already know that). Many fall into careers that cause them to work odd hours—disk jockey, actor, musician, dancer, and so on. There are a fair share of night owls by choice, too. Society as a whole is gradually switching to a twenty-four-hour day—you're just ahead of the game, as usual. Use it.

Prime time can also be a time of the year. I work better when the days are short and the weather is bad. (There are far fewer temptations then.) I try to plan my biggest projects for the dark days of winter. It works for me.

ENERGY

Self-discipline and stamina are the two major arms in a writer's arsenal.

—*Leon Uris*

Many creative people are exhausting to watch. (Robin Williams comes to mind.) They seem to possess boundless energy, enough to run an electric car or light up a city block. Most of us, though, have peaks and valleys during the day, times when our energy surges or we could use a sudden boost.

Use this chart to determine your peak energy times. (When done, you should have what looks like a wavy line.)

```
100%


50%


0
```

_____A.M.   _____NOON   _____P.M.   _____LATE NIGHT

POWER OUTAGE

You create your own propulsion for going on stage each night.

—Anthony Quinn

The effects of a lack of energy include loss of memory, trouble focusing, lack of creativity, slower reaction time, poor decision-making ability, lack of sex drive, and irritability (there may be some correlation between the last two).

What drains your energy and leaves you running on empty? Put a checkmark next to those that apply to you.

❑ Piles of unfinished work. (This is a major buzz kill. I have so much work to do, I think I'll just take a nap.)

❑ A feeling of meaninglessness or hopelessness. (Find the meaning behind what you are doing. Set goals!)

❑ Anger or turmoil. (Worry and stewing about a negative event or possible negative outcome drain energy and focus away.)

❑ Lack of exercise. (Aerobic activity can raise your energy level and boost your self-esteem.)

❑ Stress. (Meditation, long walks, a serene environment, a bath, and a massage can all help relieve stress.)

❑ A recent traumatic event. (During a crisis, you can produce enormous amounts of energy—energy you didn't know you had. You're running on adrenaline at that point. When things return to normal, your body will shut down. Take time to recharge.)

❑ Diet. (Skipping breakfast, too much sugar, and too much caffeine can affect energy levels.)

❑ Illness. (The flu, a cold, or allergies can leave you exhausted. If you're chronically tired, try cleaning your workplace to get rid of dust; be aware of other possible allergens and eliminate them.)

❑ Boredom. (Switch gears; find something new to do that will stimulate you again.)

❑ Your work environment. (An uncomfortable chair, poor lighting, clutter, a lack of privacy, even the color scheme can affect your energy level.)

❑ Everyday life. (Being busy all the time as we are, working two jobs, taking classes at night, and dealing with long commutes can take its toll.)

There is one thing noticeably missing from the foregoing list. You guessed it—lack of sleep, the number one reason for lack of energy.

SLEEP IS BETTER THAN MEDICINE

The hardest part about shooting a movie is getting up in the morning, just like any other job.

—*Brad Pitt*

To win back your waking time, get more sleep.

I feel funny writing about this, but as Mark Twain once said, "Write about what you know." I know what it's like to not get enough sleep. Like a lot of creative people, I have trouble getting to sleep and even more trouble getting enough sleep.

In my twenties I frequently pulled all-nighters. I still do in my thirties, but I pay a higher price now. I'm dragging for the next three days! So did I really get ahead or fall further behind? My philosophy used to be the more hours I was awake, the more I could accomplish. This worked for a while, but now I'm not so sure.

According to the National Sleep Council, thirty-six million Americans report that their sleep woes affect their job performance. The problem costs American businesses $18 billion annually in lack of productivity (where do they get these numbers?). Yet the main cause of sleeplessness is work: job stress, increased workload, and competition.

According to a study published in *Fortune* magazine, researchers suspect that creativity is most affected by a lack of adequate sleep. By waking up thirty minutes earlier, you can add seven and a half days to your year. But if you're sleepwalking through those seven and a half days, what have you gained?

I read in the paper about a single mom who, in an effort to provide better clothes and toys for her daughter, took a second job. After a short while, she was exhausted by her lack of sleep. During the little time she had left to spend with her daughter, she was tired and cranky. It was her daughter who wisely said, "Mommy, I don't need new clothes, I need you." Mom quit her job.

Lack of sleep over time can kill creativity. You need your z's! Let some things go so that you can get some sleep.

On the other hand, don't worry if you don't fall asleep right away. Worrying about your insomnia is a major cause of insomnia. I know people who tense up if they don't fall asleep within minutes of hitting the pillow. I enjoy that time before sleep. It can be very productive. Get comfortable, relax, turn out the light, and let your mind wander. Your brain is very receptive at this time, more open to your creative unconscious than usual. You can sort things out, get inspirations, enjoy memories of the day (or flashbacks on your life). If it takes you half an hour, an hour, or even two hours to fall asleep, that's okay.

This time can become a very important part of your day. You'll fall asleep all too soon and sleep better for it.

How to Get a Good Night's Sleep

According to a survey by Select Comfort, respondents said the best way to get a good night's sleep was the following:

1. Get a good mattress.
2. Get regular exercise. (In another study, the main reason people skipped their workout was . . . you guessed it, they were too tired. Talk about a vicious cycle!)
3. Have a quiet room and space enough to get comfortable.
4. Eat a good, well-balanced diet.
5. Sex.

Other suggestions for getting more sleep:

- Don't have a phone or a TV in the bedroom.
- Eliminate clutter in the bedroom.
- An office in the bedroom can beckon you to work.
- Too much information or stimulation close to bedtime is one of the reasons people have a hard time falling asleep.
- Go to bed when you are tired. Let your body rather than the clock tell you when to turn in.
- No caffeine or chocolate near bedtime.

NAP TIME

The time to relax is when you don't have time for it.
—*Sydney Harris*

Nearly one third of people say their job has been affected by lack of sleep. Many doze off at work. Why fight it? There is nothing like a power nap in the afternoon (no more than thirty minutes) to refresh you and give you a second wind.

On a *Seinfeld* episode, George Costanza, who on the show worked in the front office for the New York Yankees, was unable to doze off in his office because passersby could see right in. So he hired a carpenter to turn his desk into a nap center. When the carpenter was done, he could climb underneath his custom desk and curl up. There was a shelf for his alarm and a magazine rack.

I am always surprised at how refreshed I am after an afternoon siesta. Short naps (roughly twenty minutes) are best (use a timer). Sleep on a cot, bed, or couch if possible. Let's face it, for most of us, anywhere will do. While out promoting a CD, MTV's Jenny McCarthy, an obviously hyper type, was able to fall asleep anywhere, anytime—in cabs (with her feet hanging out the window), stretched out on the floor at the airport, in a chair, anywhere.

ENERGY BOOSTERS

It may seem strange to live in this world of imagery and also have a normal life. But I sleep like an angel. It is a great privilege to be able to work with, and I suppose work off, my feelings through sculpture.

—Louise Bourgeois

There are some days you can't wait to get started—everything is exciting, challenging, and interesting. Things fall into place and you hear a click, scream, "Eureka!" and are overcome by a surge of energy and enthusiasm.

Unfortunately, for most of us not all work is play, and there will be times when you need to summon the energy and get up for the task at hand. Here are several ways to boost your energy level throughout the day:

- Eat breakfast!
- Remember when a lunch hour really was an hour? In an effort to fit more in during the day, lunch is being cut back or cut out altogether. When you do break for lunch, it's not a real break. It's more like a lunch run—grab some drive-through, run a few errands, and rush back to work. It's neither relaxing nor refreshing.

- Don't eat a heavy meal. Taking several smaller snack breaks works better to keep up your blood sugar and energy levels without using all your energy for digestion. Energy bars are very good for a midmorning pick-me-up, with the benefit that they can be eaten at your desk—remember, lots of water with these! Drink lots of water anyway, to stay hydrated.

- Change your scenery. Author Jane Smiley did her writing (with her child on her lap) at restaurants. As a writer (with a laptop), I have the freedom to work wherever I choose, so I've become a regular at several different coffeehouses throughout San Diego. Duke Ellington wrote his music on trains, Alex Haley preferred to write on ships, Toni Morrison keeps a hotel room (despite having a large home) that she retreats to each day to write.

- Look at your goals and plans (or past successes)—it's an incredible energy booster. I also find that talking to my mentor is very uplifting. I can go for hours from the boost I get from talking to him.

- Discuss your project with others; get fresh ideas, input, reassurance.

- Make a change. Rearrange your office, change your hairstyle, work different hours.

- Slow down and catch up on sleep, spend some time outdoors, work out, have some fun.

- Help others, make a contribution—it will increase your self-esteem, which increases your energy.

- Change position. Some companies offer stand-up desks, which are particularly useful for jobs that require a lot of moving around.

6

• • • • •

WHEN THERE ISN'T ANY METHOD TO YOUR MADNESS

Dealing with Your Tendency to Be Late

We always hear about the haves and have-nots. Why don't we hear about the doers and the do-not's?"

— *Thomas Sowell*

If procrastination were a medical affliction, it would probably be classified as hardening of the oughteries. When we're blocked, it can be difficult to get going and even harder to push things through to completion. The stress this causes is unhealthy. But have no fear (that's one of the real reasons for procrastination); this condition is treatable, even curable.

Do you want to get well? I hope so, because procrastination, more than anything else I can think of, separates those who want to be successful from those who are. It's the difference between being a dreamer and a doer, someone who says to the world, "This is what I am going to do," then backs it up with action.

WHY WE DRAG OUR FEET

Don't put off for tomorrow what you can do today, because if you enjoy it today, you can do it again tomorrow.

—*James Michener*

Everyone procrastinates, putting off everything from changing the toilet paper roll (don't you hate that?) to putting ideas into action. Here are some of the most common reasons people put things off. Check those that apply to you.

☐ Perfectionism. If you can't do it right, you won't do it at all.

☐ You need the adrenaline rush of waiting until the last minute to get going.

☐ There is no immediate payoff for doing it now, so you postpone it while you do something that *does* have an immediate payoff.

☐ You hope it will just go away (or someone else will do it for you).

☐ You don't want to do it.

☐ You don't know how to do it. (You've never done it before.)

☐ It's boring.

☐ You're afraid of failing and looking like a fool.

☐ Low self-esteem causes you to doubt yourself and your abilities.

☐ You see yourself as above doing trivial tasks.

☐ Your environment makes it impossible to take this on right now. (No room to work, noise, distractions.)

☐ You're easily distracted and sidetracked.

☐ You're waiting for the inspiration to hit. (Then you are a "waiter" and not an artist.)

☐ You don't know where to begin.

- You're not in the mood.
- Self-sabotage and fear of success. It's a sad but real reason a lot of people procrastinate.
- There's no deadline or the deadline is distant, so you don't need to start it yet.
- You're overcommitted.
- You're waiting for the price to come down or a new model to come out.
- You can live with the results of not doing it (bad credit, poor job performance, irritated friends).

Look at the things you checked. Do you see any patterns in why you put things off?

PROCRASTINATION IN ACTION

My mother always told me I wouldn't amount to anything because I procrastinate. I said, "Just wait."

—*Judy Tenuta*

No matter what the reason, procrastination is a waste of time. If it's important enough to do it, why not do it now and get it over with? When you delay, you deprive yourself of the satisfaction and success that comes from putting ideas into action. All the talent and creativity in the world means nothing if you don't use it. If you *act (action creates triumph),* you can avoid a lot of the negative consequences that inaction creates and start to gain control of your time and your life.

So just do it—jump that first hurdle. Action begets action. If you can overcome procrastination, you've got the head start you need to see things through to completion. As the saying goes, "When you've begun, you're halfway done."

How Others "Just Did It"

TOM CLANCY:	"Just write the damn book."
IGOR STRAVINSKY:	"Just as appetite comes by eating, so work brings inspiration, if inspiration is not discernible at the beginning."
MARTIN RITT:	"Art? You just do it."
GEORGE LORIMER:	"Putting off an easy thing makes it hard, and putting off a hard one makes it impossible."
ROSANNE CASH:	"If I ignore my work, I start having anxiety attacks."
JOAN BAEZ:	"Action is the antidote to despair."
JIMMY BUFFETT:	"A lot of frustrated artists are people who didn't take the opportunity when it was presented."
TED GEISEL:	"I never leave the room during my workday, even if all I do is sit there."
MARK TWAIN:	"If you have to swallow a frog, don't stare at it too long."
JOHN UPDIKE:	"Vagueness and procrastination are ever a comfort to the frail in spirit."
WILLEM DAFOE:	"I think of myself as a doer, just someone who helps get the stuff done. That can be very exhilarating."
MARY HIGGINS CLARK:	"People say I'll start writing 'as soon as'—as soon as the kids are grown, the dog dies, whatever. I say, 'Nope, it ain't gonna happen with that attitude."
HELEN GURLEY BROWN:	"Do the rotten stuff first every day."
RED SMITH:	"Writing is easy. All you do is sit staring at the blank sheet of paper until the drops of blood form on your forehead."

MAKING MOUNTAINS OUT OF MOLEHILLS

Procrastination is a close relative of incompetence and a handmaiden of inefficiency.

—Alec MacKenzie

When you calculate the cost of delaying (wasted time, energy, and resources, not to mention stress), it seems clear that getting started is a good idea. The longer you wait, the harder it gets, the more time you spend explaining why you haven't started yet, and the more you saddle yourself with guilt. Eventually, procrastination begins to erode your credibility. It can ruin your career, damage your reputation, and cause friction in your relationships.

Worse, you shift control to others when you put things off. You become a victim. What do I mean? You are no longer in control of yourself, your career, your destiny. It's time to put yourself back in the driver's seat.

SOLUTIONS

You miss 100 percent of the shots you never take.

—Wayne Gretzky

The good news is, when you overcome procrastination, you have the power. Everything is better. The bad news is, there is no miracle drug to help. Even so, here's what I prescribe to beat the delaying disease:

- **Nibble on it.** Cut it up and break it down into bite-size pieces. Try to shove the whole thing down your throat and you will choke on it.

- **Write down two things** you have been putting off that you will follow up on. When? *Now!* Give it a start date and a deadline, and determine a first step.

- **Make a public statement.** Be accountable to someone.

- **Give it a deadline.** Advertisers know that without an expiration date, people won't act. Deadlines work. If you've been delaying cleaning up your house, schedule a party at your place. The shorter the deadline, the better. Have your boss or spouse (what's the difference there?) create deadlines for you.

- **Put the start date on your calendar,** plus specific benchmark dates for finishing pieces of the project.

- **Reward yourself** for beginning, at each step along the way and upon completion. Put the biggest reward where you need it most.

- **Worst first.** Get it over with. It gives you the burst of energy you need to finish. Think of it as a roller coaster climbing up the first section of the track. It's certainly not the fun part of the ride, but after that it's all downhill (and exhilarating).

- **Pavlov's dog.** Work on it for an hour every day—the same hour every day. When the clock strikes ten, you start. If you procrastinate, you don't get any treats.

- **List everything you have to do.** Eliminate, delegate as much as you can, mark the payoff tasks, the first step for each one, time estimates, deadlines, start times, and set aside the time to do it. By the time you've done all that junk, you'll be more than ready to jump in and get something *done.*

- **Own it, make it yours**—especially when it is something you aren't particularly excited about or have to do for someone else.

- **Ride the high.** When you're feeling good, attack the worst problems. When you're on a roll, don't stop. Ride it for all it's worth.

- **Do it quick and dirty.** Polish it when you have time.

- **Poke holes in it.** Making even a small dent in a big job motivates you to do more and overcome your initial fears.

- **Do what you are in the mood for.** Unless you're in the mood to procrastinate.

- **Do tasks you don't like** along with something you do enjoy. Exercise or clean the kitchen while you're watching your favorite TV show. Study for a test while getting a massage (this works for only about the first fifteen to twenty minutes).

- **Delegate some of it.** Barter. You might be surprised to find that your co-worker loves to compile figures and hates to draw graphs. Work together.

- **Simplify it.** Eliminating part of a task gives you a jump start on the rest.

- **Limit yourself.** Sit at your work space and do nothing, or just sit and doodle, but don't allow yourself to do anything other than work on the project at hand. Don't answer the phone, don't talk to anybody, don't read. Eventually you will be itching to begin.

- **Change your environment.** The worst things seem better in better light, a more comfortable chair, a rich green room. Or just take it outdoors, to a coffee shop, or home.

- **If you don't know how, ask!** Research it. Talk to those who have done it. Get input and ideas. Follow in their footsteps. You don't have to reinvent the wheel, and you don't have to do it perfect the first time.

- **Get help!** Hire a personal trainer or a U.S. Marine Corps sergeant to get you going.

- **Use synergy.** Surround yourself with high-energy people. It rubs off.

- **Know your weaknesses and work around them.** Use your peak energy times to begin.

- **Try Method acting.** Find the motivation, slip into the role of an achiever—and boom! you're getting things done.

- **Have a goal.** Jack Canfield and Mark Victor Hansen, authors of the *Chicken Soup for the Soul* books, have a goal to land one TV, radio, or print interview a day.

- **Gather everything you need** to do the project before you start. The act of pulling this together itself can get you started.

- **Start on a positive note.** Do some small part of the project that you can easily complete.

- **Hit the ground running.** Try using a template to give you the head start you need to begin. You can add ideas and personalize as you go.

- **Brainstorm**—and carry the energy that creates right into starting the project. Don't pause, don't slow down. Milk that inspiration. When it runs out, you can go back and clean up, reflect, polish.

- **Lower the bar.** Practice working with no expectations. Don't let preconceived ideas stop you from doing anything.

- **Jump in anywhere.** Start in the middle. Do it in any order you want.

- **Be positive.** "I am enjoying cleaning my house. I am positively enjoying this opportunity to scrub." (This one's a stretch for even the most imaginative, but you can do it!)

- **Just freakin' do it!** It's amazing how easy things are once you begin. The faster you start, the quicker you'll get done. (Now I sound like my mother. Aaaaauuuuugh!)

PERFECTIONIST QUIZ

Perfectionism goes hand in hand with procrastination. Are you a perfectionist?

1. Do you never feel like something is finished?

2. Are you your own harshest critic? Do you get disgusted with others for not demanding more from you?

3. Do you always give people more than they expect (or need or want)?

4. Do you frequently turn things in late, always needing just a little more time to get them "just right"?

5. Do people say you don't know when to quit?

6. Do you give everything you do the same amount of attention, regardless of how important it is?

7. Do you have a reputation as being hard to please? Are you proud of that reputation?

8. Do you interfere with your co-workers/partners, frequently redoing their work to your specifications?

9. Are you competitive to the point where you can't quit until you've won?

10. Do you have negative feelings about your body, hair, voice?

11. Do you rewrite family letters and interoffice memos two and three times before you send them?

12. Do you frequently apologize for the inadequacy of your work, your home, your car, your children, and the like?

13. Do you feel compelled to mention every single detail when telling a story, making a presentation, or filing a report?

14. If you don't do everything on your "to do" list, do you feel like a failure?

15. Do you have trouble delegating because "it would be easier to do it myself"?

16. Do you have trouble going to a car wash, using a gardener, or hiring (and keeping) a housekeeper?

17. Have you hurt or angered people you care about because you can't stop picking on them?

18. Do you spend hours on trivial details and then feel resentful that people don't notice how perfectly the page numbers line up?

19. Do you have trouble with relationships?

20. Do you focus on the one less than perfect review and ignore dozens of good ones? (I can recite mine verbatim.)

TRYING TO BE PERFECT IN AN IMPERFECT WORLD

I did my best, but I guess my best wasn't good enough. I gave my all, but I guess my all was too much.

—*James Ingram*

There is no such thing as perfection. Seeking it only leads to futility and frustration. It's a battle you can't win and isn't worth trying for anyway. To try to live a perfect life is destructive and debilitating. You will never feel that you are good enough, that your work is finished. You'll feel like a failure, which leads to procrastination. Why even try?

Over time, the stress of trying to be perfect takes its toll. You're tired, overworked, and disappointed. Always being on, trying to reach unattainable ideals, always feeling like a failure . . . This is no way to live. It squashes your creativity. Trust me, I know. Perfection and procrastination go hand in hand. And both of them stunt your natural creative talents.

WHEN GOOD ENOUGH IS GOOD ENOUGH

Too much polishing weakens rather than improves a work.

—*Pliny the Younger*

Who says you have to do anything perfectly? You? Anybody else? If there's anybody in your life (besides yourself) telling you that you have to do everything perfectly the first time, get away from that person right now. If it's your supervisor, change jobs. I mean it. If it's your mother, move out. Be polite, be firm, hang up. Just don't listen, because it's a lot of hooey.

You learn more from your failures than from your successes. If you're not allowed to fail, you're never going to learn, you'll never develop the ability to deal with problems, you'll stunt your personal, professional, and creative growth. Besides, everybody hates perfect people. That's why I've always tried to be not quite perfect myself (and I'm succeeding, too).

Program yourself to accept imperfection:

- **Tell yourself you will feel good about accomplishing this today.**

- **Ask yourself:** Will the results be that much better if I put in more effort? Will anyone notice? If the answer is "no," cut yourself some slack.

- **How much is this job worth** (sorting the mail, cleaning the bathroom, this project or report)? If you pay yourself an hourly rate based on the value of your time, how many hours can you afford to spend on this one thing?

- **Be in the moment.** "Do not fear mistakes. There are none," said the late Miles Davis. Jazz music is improvisational in its nature, and that's what makes it so great. It's not about achieving perfection, but rather about being in the moment and playing what feels right.

- **Don't sweat the small stuff.** Pick your spots to shine in.

- **Cut your co-worker/partner/kid some slack.** Learn to value each person's unique style and perspective. Think of them as jazz notes.

- **Focus on the big picture.** The fact that the frosting on the wedding cake is pink instead of peach becomes less important when you focus on the fact that you're going to spend the rest of your life with this wonderful person beside you.

- **Learn to live with your shortcomings.** Stephen J. Cannell has written for and produced many of the shows on TV today. Because of dyslexia, he flunked several grades and grew up thinking he was stupid. He admits that to this day his spelling is atrocious. But he doesn't care. "I know writers who agonize over their writing. I don't. I think the writers who agonize over their writing are preoccupied with the idea of being perfect—and brilliant. I decided I'm not going to spend my life trying to learn to spell 'complete.' I just write it the way it comes out best."

- **Just keep going.** Going back to correct as you go is a mistake when writing or painting. It kills the flow, frustrates creativity. Let it pour out without your self-critic getting in the way.

- **Trust your gut.** As a director, Clint Eastwood is known for working quickly, completing projects on time, and producing quality work. He says, "You have to trust your instincts. There's a moment when an actor has it, and he knows it."

- **Leave it to the experts.** Anne Lamott, author of *Bird by Bird,* recommends that writers create what she calls "a shitty first draft." Leave all the warts on it at this point, correct later (or what's an editor for?).

- **Concentrate on the work itself.** Don't focus so much on what others will think or say when you're done. You can't control the responses of others, but I can guarantee that if you don't finish or finish late, you will get a negative response.

- **There are no bad decisions.** Except no decision at all.

- **Compromise.** Create the best work you can and struggle with the reality that you have to sell it.

- **Competent vs. perfect.** Which is better, to turn in complete and competent work on time or incomplete, perfect work that is late? It's generally better to be productive than perfect.

MOTIVATION

The force is within you—force yourself.
—Harrison Ford

Many times action precedes motivation, not the other way around. The motivation to do something comes from within. It is a mistake to wait for inspiration to begin working on something. Working on it will provide the spark that lights the fire.

"The great composer does not set to work because he is inspired, but becomes inspired because he is working. Beethoven, Bach, and Mozart settled down day after day to the job at hand with as much regularity as an accountant settles down each day to his figures. They didn't waste time waiting for inspiration," Ernest Newman said. It's true for any creative. Experienced and successful creative people don't believe as much in inspiration as they do in perspiration and self-motivation.

MOTIVATION BOOSTERS

One of the things I learned the hard way was that it doesn't pay to get discouraged. Keeping busy and making optimism a way of life can restore your faith in yourself.
—Lucille Ball

If you feel unmotivated and are having a hard time getting started, consider this list of motivation boosters:

- **Follow through on what you start,** and do what you say you're going to do. Make it a point of honor and be proud of it.

- **Make some changes.** Redecorate, change your look, change your salutation. (When someone says, *"How are you?"* what do you say? Instead of saying, "I'm alive, aren't I?" try, "I'm fantastic," or, "I'm better than great."

- **Fake it till you make it.** Act as if you are already successful (without the attitude, please).

- **Take responsibility for your actions**—and your mistakes. If you can't admit you made a mistake, you can't learn from it. *That's* a mistake.

- **Don't talk about your problems with strangers.**

- **Start a support group,** networking club, or mastermind group.

- **Don't overgeneralize your weaknesses or situation** ("I can't draw.") "I can't draw a horse" gives you a place to start. If you want to draw a horse, take a class or buy a drawing book about horses.

- **Help others, give back, volunteer.** Focusing on others' needs helps you feel better about yourself and boosts your motivation.

- **Find a role model** or mentor you can turn to for advice and support.

- **Go one week without criticizing,** complaining, or condemning.

- **Smile.** A lot.

- **Use affirmations.** "I'm good enough the way I am" (and, doggone it, people *like* me).

- **List the mistakes you think you made in the last year** and what you learned from each. Don't stop working on this one until you have learned a lesson from every mistake.

- **Put up signs that say "Yes!"** all over your house.

- **Take action.** If something is eating at you, write a letter, call your congressperson or your mother (won't she be surprised!).

- **Make a list of things that bother you.** Next to each item, write down what you are going to do about it. Don't leave any blanks.

- **Send yourself fan mail or flowers.** Leave nice messages on your own answering machine. Make a scrapbook or collage of your best work, places you've been, photos of friends.

BETTER LATE THAN NEVER

Fashionably late is an oxymoron.

—*Ms. Manners*

Lateness says a lot about you. It says "selfish, disinterested, incompetent, unreliable, unprofessional, out of control, unprepared, desperate."

Being late is not the problem, however. The real problem is the effect it has. Running late can (and does) cause you stress, whether you admit it or not. Chronic lateness wreaks havoc on everyone around you. (They are usually more peeved than they let on.) You can lose respect, jobs, clients, lovers, and friends over lateness. *That's* a problem.

Being early, or at least on time, eliminates a lot of time management problems. It's one giant step to getting a handle on your time—and your life.

WHY WE ARE A DAY LATE AND A DOLLAR SHORT

I've been on a calendar but never on time.

—*Marilyn Monroe*

Creative people can come up with some creative excuses for being late. "It was so hot today that the asphalt molecules in the highway expanded, creating a greater distance between my house and the office." "You mean Halloween isn't a national holiday?" "I lost my American Express card and I couldn't leave home without it."

Some of the real reasons behind chronic lateness include the following:

- **Self-sabotage.** You don't think you deserve success, so you show up late for job interviews or auditions or don't finish projects on time. Fear driven, this is one of those self-fulfilling prophecies.

- **You like working under pressure** and underestimate how long things will take to complete.

- **You accept projects with competing deadlines.**

- **You're unrealistic about time.** If a meeting is thirty miles away, it should take thirty minutes to get there, right? Wrong! Not even if you have a helicopter.

- **You lose focus or get distracted.** You just have to squeeze in one more thing before leaving. You can't resist answering the phone even though you're on the way out the door.

- **You pick inappropriate times to do things**—ten minutes before you're supposed to leave, you start cleaning out the medicine cabinet, which you noticed was a mess while searching for your eyeliner.

- **You get lost in a project or a book or a TV show** and forget about a meeting or a deadline until too late.

- **You still have time.** Every year on April 15 (tax time), I watch the news with morbid fascination as they show the long lines of cars full of people waiting to drop off their tax forms at the main post office (which stays open till midnight) so they get their returns postmarked on time. Thirty million people wait until the last minute to file their returns. You don't have to be one of them.

- **There is no immediate payoff.** Which is why rewarding yourself works so well.

- **Defiance, rebellion, or indifference** are not so hidden reasons behind chronic lateness. There is power in making people wait.

- **You rely on others** to tell you when to be somewhere or when something is due. Then you have someone to blame. "You were supposed to remind me about our meeting."

HOW TO BE ON TIME, EVERY TIME

I never could have done what I have done without the habit of punctuality, order, and diligence.
—*Charles Dickens*

Someone once pointed out that punctuality is the art of guessing how late the other person will be. There's some truth in that. There are many more concrete methods for avoiding lateness, however. After working until the wee hours of the morning on a computer problem, my brother decided to sleep on the couch, since we had to leave for work first thing in the morning and he didn't trust me to wake him up. So he asked for and guzzled down several glasses of water. His reasoning: His bladder would wake him up on time.

When I am on the road doing seminars, I ask the hotel operator to give me three wake-up calls about ten minutes apart. (I'm used to having a snooze alarm at home.)

Other techniques you might want to try:

- **Use a timer or alarm** to remind you when you have to leave for an appointment.

- **Put off your distractions.** If you are preparing to leave and you see something that needs to be done, write it on a Post-it note and come back to it later.

- **Try to arrive early.** Don't laugh. I have a friend who hates to be early as much as she hates to be late. She always plans to be exactly on time, but if something unforeseen happens (like unusually bad traffic), she's late—and totally stressed out.

- **Set your watch and clocks ahead five minutes.**

- **Remind your partner.** If you and another person are driving together to a meeting or appointment, call the person to confirm a day or two before the date.

- **Be considerate.** If you know in advance you are going to be late, call and warn the party who will be waiting.

- **Put a clock in the bathroom.**

- **Write appointments in your calendar** for a half hour earlier than they really are. My wife's mother used to tell my sister-in-law that holiday dinners were an hour earlier than actually planned. That way she was only an hour late.

- **Anticipate problems.** If you are often late because of someone else, anticipate them being late and plan for it. Or go separately and meet there.

- **Streamline the process of getting ready.** Set out everything you need to take with you the night before so you can grab and go.

- **Know yourself.** If you're not a morning person, don't schedule a meeting at seven A.M.

- **Get detailed directions.**

- **Time yourself.** Things always take longer than you think. How much time does it really take you to get ready? Timing yourself can be a real eye-opener.

- **Get organized.** (Looking for lost things is a big reason for being late.) Keep a set of spare keys handy.

- **Eliminate distractions** when getting ready to leave. TV is like a magnet, pulling you in and mesmerizing you for minutes at a time.

- **Bring reading material with you** and make use of the time if you have to wait. Then being early becomes a blessing instead of a hassle.

- **Apologize.** If you are late for a lunch meeting, offer to buy. After a few times of having to do this, you should have some real motivation to break the late habit.

- **Put the alarm on the other side of the room** if you abuse the snooze.

- **Keep your gas tank halfway full,** saving the time it takes to fill up when you are already running late.
- **Leave a buffer between meetings** in case one runs over. Keep a timer or beeper in your pocket or purse set to go off at a specific time so you are reminded to leave in time to make your next meeting.

HOW TO SEE THINGS THROUGH TO COMPLETION

Without discipline, there's no life at all.
—Katharine Hepburn

I've done it! What a great feeling that is. You want to scream and dance and run naked in the streets. (Sorry, I got a little carried away there.) When you can point to the scoreboard and say, "I am a winner," it's a feeling like no other. And the perks that come with it, ah! Raises, promotions, bonuses, and, my personal favorite, respect and admiration. To be a successful creative person takes natural ability, talent, and the self-discipline and commitment to overcome temptation, procrastination, and rejection. You must do, try, finish, and follow through to succeed. You are judged by what you do (your actions)—and also by what you don't do. Be a doer.

- **Make fewer promises** and keep the ones you make. Whenever you keep your word and do what you say you will do, you increase the equity in your integrity and self-worth accounts.
- **Form a mastermind group** of four to six people you respect. People who know what you're trying to do can help you along the way and will hold you accountable for finishing what you start.
- **Make finishing things a habit.** It may seem difficult at first, but after following through on the little things, day by day, you will find it becomes second nature. Seeing your completed book on the shelf, your play up on

the stage, your artwork in a gallery . . . it's positively addicting.

- **Work like the devil,** and move heaven and earth if you have to, but don't focus on the work—focus on the result. Reward yourself when you are finally done.

- **Make a list of all your unfinished business.** This helps to put things into perspective. Divide it up into categories. Drop what you can. Choose a "most wanted" list of the top five things you will complete, no matter what. Start working on one today and do a little each day until it's done.

- **Do the best you can with what you have.** Waiting for the right moment, the right tools, the right circumstances to begin can be an excuse for procrastination. Do it now!

- **The future will take care of itself.** If the reason you don't finish things is that you don't know what you'll do next, trust that more and better projects will come your way as long as you follow through.

- **Use humor to ease the pressure.** In the book *Organizing for the Creative Person,* the authors share one woman's method for encouraging action. She carried around a file labeled "Today, dammit!"

- **Write a contract with yourself** stating your intentions and outlining what you'll do and when you'll do it. Have someone mail copies of this letter to you at thirty-day intervals—or until you are done.

- **Leave things out in plain sight.** It's one way to remember to work on, and complete, various projects and tasks.

- **Find the passion in what you're doing** (hint, the purpose), and you will be charged to finish it.

- **Slip the tasks you don't like between the ones you do.** Alternate among the good, bad, and ugly things you usually have to do in order to finish something.

- **Do as much as you can at a time.** There is a quote I like by Neil Fiore: "All tasks are completed in a series of starts and stops." Sure, everyone wants to hit a home run, but you can score lots of runs by hitting singles and doubles.

- **And, as Winston Churchill said, "Never, never, never quit."**

7

·····

"PILE" CABINETS, PLANNERS, AND POST-IT NOTES

Tools You Can Use

The trouble with being in the rat race is that even if you win, you're still a rat.

—*Lily Tomlin*

There is no denying that life is faster and more chaotic than ever. You are forced to juggle more things at once with more details to remember, more things to do, calls to make, and, as a result, more little hand-scrawled scraps of paper everywhere. Important reminders and information can get lost, misplaced, and forgotten. This can be embarrassing, damage your reputation, or, worse, cause others to lose faith in you.

When who you know is more important than what you know, keeping track of all the people in your life is vital. Once upon a time, you maybe had an address and two phone numbers for people. Now you have fax numbers, pager numbers, e-mail addresses, cellular phones, home and work numbers, and more. The old Hallmark calendar and little black book just don't work anymore.

Fortunately there are modern solutions to these modern challenges, tools that can help you to get a grip. Really. There has to be a better way.

Skeptical that any tool out there could actually make managing your time and tasks any easier? Good. No tool can completely manage your time and tasks for you—only *you* can do that. Still, nothing says you can't make it as easy on yourself as possible. Planners, personal information managers, and software designed to save your time can end up being more trouble than they are worth, so look for tools that are easy to learn, easy to use, easy to implement, and don't require you to change the way you live your life.

I rounded up and reviewed *everything* I could find, searching for tools that can really make a difference without a lot of fuss and muss. The following tools—both high- and low-tech—are fun, flexible, and user-friendly (not to mention highly functional). In short, these are tools that won't further complicate your life, stifle your creativity, and/or take away your spontaneity. All have one thing in common: using one or more of them can make day-to-day living a tiny bit easier.

WHAT WON'T WORK

If a system or tool goes against your natural style of doing things, it's likely that you'll find it awkward, become frustrated, and abandon the whole thing. If it takes too long to learn, set up, and use, the product becomes a time-waster instead of a time-saver. I tried to narrow down the many tools out there to those with a better chance of working without a lifestyle change, a crisis of personality, or a complete overhaul of how you manage your day and live your life.

I realize that across-the-board solutions won't work. Everyone has individual preferences. I'll provide several different approaches in this chapter, some of them mutually exclusive; you decide what would be best for your situation and your style of doing things. Don't be afraid to design your own system rather than buy a prefabricated one.

New, high-tech solutions for time management are coming on the market every day, but new isn't always better. Sometimes the old-fashioned, paper-based method is best. Don't be fooled into thinking that you have to buy every new product that comes out or upgrade old ones just because they are there. Trying to keep up is a waste of time—and money.

Most of the products out there for managing time are somewhat inflexible and cumbersome. Many of these systems were designed for people who already lead structured, compartmentalized, and, quite frankly, boring lives. A noncreative person wouldn't think twice about making a list, checking it twice, then organizing it into A, B, and C priorities (am I scaring you?). This is not a natural thing for the creative person. You feel constricted by this linear, step-by-step approach and quickly give up. There *are* tools that will work for you, however, tools that allow you to be the flexible, lovable, creative person you are—and get a handle on things, too.

● ●

How Do You See the Year?

How do you see time? How do you see the year? month? day? Some see the year, for instance, as a clockwise circle, others with the months in a straight line moving from left to right. Still others see the year as a traditional calendar that is laid out. My editor says she sees the year as a mountain to climb. Find tools that match your vision, or create your own.

● ●

WHAT WORKS!

The basic premise behind the following tools is that they can make your life easier and free you up to be more creative and spontaneous. Yes, you read that right. *Spontaneous.*

Try one or two things and implement them until they become a habit. A simple system is likely to work best, one that is creative, colorful, and at the very least includes a calendar. A "to do" list, calendar, and address book are enough for many; others will need more complex solutions. The key is deciding what and how much you want to (and must) get done. Then you can find the best tools to help you do it without a lot of extra work.

The goal is to do some planning but still remain flexible—to make it to meetings, find information fast, record ideas, and lose less stuff.

POST-IT NOTES

In the years since 3M scientist Art Fry invented the Post-it note, it has become one of the five best-selling office products in the United States. There are more than 250 Post-it products, from the original pastel yellow pads to bright neon colors to notes shaped like feet (foot notes?) to notes that smell like pizza, to big Easel Pads, to repositional wall decorations for a child's bedroom (it's never too early to start a kid on Post-it notes).

This little yellow sticky thing has become the creative person's best friend, a key weapon in our arsenal against the onslaught of little bits of information. So simple, yet so effective. I see nothing wrong with Post-it notes plastered all over your office, your home, your car—as long as every once in a while you remove the outdated ones.

There is no wrong way to use a Post-it note. They inspire creativity. Their key advantage is in their ability to stick cleanly to files (or piles) of papers, planners, banners, memos, demos, phones, walls, stalls, doors, floors, chairs, or computer screens.

THE MANY USES OF POST-IT NOTES (SOME YOU NEVER THOUGHT OF)

MESSAGES. I leave notes to my wife on the fridge: "Your mother called and said she'll be over at six. I decided to go to the ball game after all." Notes to myself on the door: "Leave house no later than 5:30!!!" Notes to the neighbor on his car: "Change of plan, leaving early for game." Another reminder to myself on the dash of my car: "Don't forget tickets on dresser."

BOOKMARKS. Put a marker in the Yellow Pages directory for frequently needed information. Mark the favorite passages of a book. Affix directions to a map as a reminder for future trips to that area. Leave a note to yourself if you're interrupted while working on a project. Put down where you are and where you were going, so when you come back, you can pick up right where you left off.

"TO DO" LIST. I first came across this in Ann McGee-Cooper's book, *Time Management for Unmanageable People.* On a freestanding board, wall board, or card stock, you can organize things to do by urgency, mood, or category, and move them around as the day or week progresses. For instance, give yourself three columns by folding a piece of card stock in three. One could be "Calls," another "Appointments," and a third "Things to Do." You could divide it horizontally into "Family," "Work," and "Me." Or keep it simple and make your three columns "Things to Do," "Doing," "Done." You get the picture. Add new tasks as they arise or you remember them. At the end of the day, peel off completed tasks.

ON A CALENDAR. Use Post-it notes to arrange appointments, meetings, or calls on the tentative day. As things change, move the Post-it note to the appropriate day. I made a "to do" list that looked like a board game and moved my little Post-it notes around on the board. You could make a racetrack and race them around. I told a friend about this, and the next day he created what looked like a battlefield, with Post-it notes lined up like little soldiers, each with their orders.

REMINDERS. Print customized checklists on Post-it notes (you can now run them through your inkjet or laser printer). You know how a pilot runs through a series check before taking off? You can do the same before leaving the house. Stick these reminders to your purse, keys, the door. "Remember to turn off the coffeemaker, feed dog," and so on.

Use Post-it notes to help you establish a habit by reminding you every day in appropriate places to use the new tool or technique. Stick extra ones in the bathroom where you'll see them at your leisure.

EDUCATION. I try to learn a new word every day. I tack the word-of-the-day ("ululate") on my mirror, with its meaning ("to hoot and howl"), and try to use it in a sentence while shaving. "When I cut myself with the razor, I ululated."

BUSINESS TOOL. Flags; minifax cover sheets; custom-made pads with company logo, address, and phone/fax numbers; informal pads with your name, phone/fax, and e-mail numbers for quick memos; routing slips; Easel pads (twenty-five by thirty inches) for presentations and signs; meeting notices; memos; telephone messages—all come in useful. If the copy machine breaks, you can put an out-of-order sign on it with a note about when it will be fixed. If you're out to lunch, you can leave a note on your door or computer screen saying how you can be reached or when you'll be back. Print a cartoon or quote or drawing along with your business card information on them and hand out pads as a guerrilla marketing tactic.

OTHER. I have used them as you would bread crumbs, making arrows directing people to my seminar room in large hotels. *Dilbert* creator Scott Adams uses them as toys to entertain his cats. On a wall map, I stick errands and meetings, trying to group them together geographically and plan my day that way.

In the novel *Longshot* by Dick Francis, the lead character is a survival expert who always carries Post-it notes with him as a survival tool, handy for making maps, marking a trail, and helping to start a fire.

One woman puts notes on things like the ice tray her husband left on the counter: "I'm not a magic ice tray. Don't expect me to refill myself." Or the cereal boxes left out: "I can't fly. Can you put me back in the cupboard?" For dirty socks left around: "I don't have legs. Will you put me in the hamper?" After years of nagging, this finally did the trick.

POST-IT SOFTWARE

If you ever wondered how we got by without paper Post-it notes, you'll love the electronic version. That's right, there is an electronic version that works much like the paper kind. You can sprinkle brightly colored digital Post-it notes *inside* your computer with the same ease and convenience you get from the paper kind. Jot down your thoughts and reminders, then file them, print them, or send them to others.

It's as easy to do as it sounds. Organize your notes by project or subject, create notes while working in any document or application, and find these stored notes with the "find" feature. You can even set alarms to prevent notes and appointments from being lost or forgotten. The feature I like best is that you don't have to open a new program to make a note to yourself. You can make lists with your notes; set alarms to go off at the beginning of the day to remind you to look at appointments; create memo boards to store phone numbers, deadlines, and to-do's for each project; color code your notes; and search by key words.

For Macintosh users, there's a shareware program called Stickies that you open from the Apple menu, any time, from inside any application. A little yellow pad comes on your screen and you can type in your note, positioning it anywhere on your screen. While it doesn't have all the features of the Post-it notes version, it does give you a quick, cheap, and easy way to leave notes to yourself or somebody else computer style.

TABLE SCRAPS

Arrange whatever pieces come your way.
—*Virginia Woolf*

In a television interview, writer Anne Rice freely admits to leaving notes to herself everywhere. She writes on the wall, the floor, the radio. I guess that's what you would call freedom of expression.

Can't break the habit of writing things on little scraps of paper or whatever's handy (matchbooks, napkins, envelopes, bills, or any semipermeable surface within reach)? There's nothing inherently wrong with this technique, except that if you wrote a note on your palm and wash your hand before copying it down somewhere more permanent, it's lost forever. One photographer liked to scribble important phone numbers on the wall next to the phone to save time looking them up. Then one day an overzealous janitor scrubbed them all off.

If you insist on the scribble-it system, try this:

- **Use both sides** when you're making a note on a scrap of paper or envelope. That way you have a much better chance of finding the note when you need it, and a lesser chance you'll toss it by mistake.

- **Make notes on full-size sheets of paper** and stick them onto your copy board or into the file of the relevant project. Don't worry about wasting a whole sheet for one small note. At least it won't get lost or crumpled, and you can always add more to the page later.

- **Buy a planner** or notebook that has a pocket to keep your scraps of paper in.

- **A string-tie type** of clear or translucent plastic letter-size envelope is good for keeping scraps of paper. A clear check organizer can be used to sort scraps by month, category, project, whatever.

- **Scribble on Post-it notes** and stick them on a bulletin board.

- **A photo album with sticky pages can be used to secure notes,** but it's a pain to take them in and out because of the plastic overlay.

- **Pegboard or corkboard an entire wall for notes.** If you set up categories and stick your notes under category headings, it'll be much easier to find what you need later.

- **Scribble your notes on a steno pad.** Write a starting date big on the cover, write all your bits of information on the one pad until it's full, and write a "full up" date big on the cover. You can file these or stick them in a drawer. When you need to find a note about somebody you spoke to in September 1977, you'll know basically where to look.

- **Keep a fishbowl or in-box for scraps**—a dump site, as it were. Go through the scraps and review often, transferring important numbers into your phone file and tossing what you no longer need.

- **Staple scraps to larger paper or card stock for saving,** or staple them to dates in your planner or calendar.

- **Make a "to do" list from your scraps.** If it looks like a ransom note, so what?

- **Scan the most important scribbles into your computer** for a more permanent record. Create a "Scraps" file. This sounds cool, but it can cost way more in time and computer memory than it's worth.

- **Use a permanent marker** if you write on your palm or the wall!

BETTER SOLUTIONS

If you don't run your own life, somebody else will.
—John Atkinson

There are better systems, especially in the follow-up and reminder areas. Many a lost scrap can cause you to miss a deadline, forget a meeting, fail to send out vital information. What follows are some more conventional (and creative) solutions.

ROLODEX

In my hometown, the owner of an escort service was arrested, and the key piece of evidence against her was her Rolodex. She quickly became known as "the Rolodex madam." I would guess many of us run our businesses using a Rolodex as our primary networking tool.

There's nothing wrong with the old faithful Rolodex card files—unless you keep incriminating evidence on them. Use the bigger format cards, so all you have to do is staple or paste on a business card and make a couple of notes. Classic, simple to use, easy to update. People keep recipes, emergency numbers, serial numbers, combinations to locks, and computer shortcuts on their Rolodex, in addition to phone, fax, e-mail, and URL addresses.

Rolodex also makes electronic organizers in a number of sizes. The most intriguing is the DataPage. This little thing fits in most planners (not much thicker than a page or two), can hold all your contact information, and is a scheduler, clock, alarm, and calculator. Like most Rolodex products, it is simple to use and has a clean design (with a neat little raised rubber keypad).

Rolodex Personal Organizers live up to the company's slogan, "Keep it simple." It looks good, too, is affordable and available in four sizes, and comes with a Post-it note dispenser built right in. They get it!

INDEX CARDS

A software program called TakeNote is an electronic version of an index card. The good old paper version works best for me, though. I use them all the time.

- **Put ideas on index cards,** or use them for notes—one subject per card.

- **Save old ideas,** lists, projects, in a file box.

- **Use cards as bookmarks.** If you see something you can use or want to remember while you're reading, write it on that card. Things you'll implement! (Try it with this book.)

- **When planning a project,** put ideas or tasks on cards and shuffle them as things change.

- **Use different-colored cards** for phone, urgent, appointments, and the like.

- **Pin them on the wall** as reminders or to outline the day, a speech, a paper.

PLANNERS

Many people keep their whole lives in their planner. It's the one place they turn to for stuff that shouldn't be left up to memory alone (appointment dates, times, directions, contact persons, phone numbers, notes). A planner allows you to keep everything in one place and take it with you. Information is portable and easy to find.

The best part about a planner is that there is no right or wrong way to use one. Organize it any way you want, use whatever symbols you want, put sections in any order that makes sense to you.

- **Choose one that's big enough to hold everything** and compact enough to take with you. (Tip: Buy a planner that your kid could carry or that you could carry while also carrying a briefcase, purse, seven file folders, and an overcoat *and* wearing three-inch heels.)

- **Simplify.** If the one you like best is filled with things you'll never use, take them out. Think of it as your mobile command center—functional, functional, functional.

- **Specialize.** There are planners designed especially for students to keep track of their busy schedules, for homemakers to keep shopping lists, recipes, kid's schedules, appointments, and tips. Try to find one with the specialized forms you need.

- **Link it.** You might want to consider a planner that's linked to computer calendar software. These let you print out your address book or calendar in a size and format that slips right into your planner.

- **Binder systems work best**—you can move things around and add pages when you need them.

- **Get the right style.** Your planner should have enough space and appropriate places to put your information so you can keep everything running smoothly, even when you have a million things going at once. If there's not enough room on a monthly planner, switch to a larger format or a weekly planner.

Being able to write things down and find them again frees up your mind for other pursuits. An all-in-one system that includes everything you'll need to run your day—a calendar, phone numbers, "to do" list and whatever else you'll need—keeps things simple and eliminates hunting for a note or going back for something you forgot or doing without something you need.

The best thing about paper-based planners is that it takes no time at all to learn to use them. And no batteries are required! You don't have to turn it on or plug it in to make it work. It's easily accessible and inexpensive, and unlike your laptop, nobody's likely to steal it.

The downside, which is easily offset by the tremendous upside, is that you have to do everything manually (as opposed to an electronic version that automatically moves birthdays from year to year, for instance). There is no "key word" function to search through and index your notes, no reminder alarms, not as many color graphics, no autodial. Even so, it's still the best bet for most creative people.

Planners come in weekly, monthly, and daily styles. Most creative people like a weekly view, not too long-term, not too anal. Here are some things you might want to look for when choosing a planner:

- **Post-it notes holder,** very handy.
- **A place to keep quotes,** conversions, city abbreviations, maps, zip codes, special dates, and holidays.
- **Pockets** for loose papers, receipt holders.
- **Zip pockets** to hold emergency supplies and pens.
- **The best ones open and lie flat**—easier to write in and refer to on your desk.
- **Zipper closure** to keep loose papers from falling out.
- **Pages with space** to draw, doodle, and design, a section of blank pages, or a notepad.

- **A small calculator** or electronic organizer.
- **Address pages** should include room for e-mail, Internet address, voice mail, pager.
- **Size *is* important:** you need room to write or draw, while maintaining portability.
- **Good looks.** Get one you like the look of, one you'd be proud to carry.
- **New voice-mail record sheets** are a handy innovation: these provide a place to write down your phone messages.
- **Calendars** for at least three years ahead.
- **Business card holders,** diskette holders.
- **Custom tabs.**
- **A section for big projects** with room to add information/inspirations.
- **A "things to do" list.**
- **A place to stick invoices,** expense forms, other forms you need to fill out.

Whatever planner you choose:
- **Use only one planner** for both personal and professional needs.
- **Have a backup for important information** (phone numbers, especially) in case, God forbid, your planner is lost.
- **Get rid of bulky stuff you don't need or use.** Mine is a bit on the hefty side and because it contains my checkbook I get tired of hauling it around. Someday soon I'm going to pare it down. Real soon.
- **Fill in regular events,** like weekly staff meetings, birthdays, and anniversaries, in advance.
- **Make it fun.** Use stickers, colored pens.
- **Leave your planner open on your desk** and refer to it during the day.

- **Build in some leeway.** When entering appointments, enter the time you should leave to get there and any items to bring with you. I also write down the address and phone number with the appointment time for quick reference.

MAKE YOUR OWN

If you can't find the perfect planner, or if prefabricated planners don't appeal to you, make your own. With desktop publishing and your creativity, you can design a custom planner that works just the way you want it to. All the supplies you need are available at most office supply or art supply stores. Binders or leather cases (simulated leather, if you choose to go the frugal route) should be in standard ring sizes so you can put other notes and papers in your planner easily and without a special hole punch. Calendars, stand-alone "things to do" lists, tabs you can customize into categories of your choosing, lined paper, colored paper, pocket dividers, Post-it note holders, zipper bags for loose change, stamps, office supplies, colored pens, stickers. Notepad or sketchpad for journaling your thoughts or taking meeting notes. Picture holders, diskette holders, calculators, check registers, rulers, address holders, business card pockets. Or you can use the best sections of some of the mass-market planners and develop your own additions. The biggest advantage I found was that when you make your own, you can make it fun! Add color, a crazy format, a left-handed version, whatever you want.

MY PLANNER

I'm a list maker; I'm a bit anal that way.
—*George Carlin*

Since I am obviously "pro-planner," I thought it would be only fair to share how I use mine, how I custom-designed it to fit my own needs, and what's in it.

I created a page to keep track of the things I have loaned out. It's one thing to put your name inside a book, "Property of Lee Silber"—and quite another to get it back. Oprah had a whole show about people who borrowed things and never returned them and the guilt they felt. One woman borrowed a typewriter and finally returned it—fifteen years later! Another borrowed a lawn mower, broke it, and never picked it up from the repair shop.

I created a page to capture all the nice things people say about me (and a pocket page for "fan" letters). Whenever someone says, "Boy, you look like you've lost weight," or, "I loved your last book," I note it down. When I feel particularly blue, I read through these notes for a quick pick-me-up.

I also devoted space for goals. I created mini–goal boards that include my written-out goals and a picture or magazine clipping to visually represent each goal. I refer to this section each morning to help me stay focused and committed to the big picture.

- An idea catcher (page and pocket) to write down ideas for stories, quotes, facts, products. I will often hear something that would be useful in one of my books. I tear out articles, pick up things for my idea files, and so forth.

- My calendar is a monthly two-page spread, with a column down the far right side for the most important things to do this month. I will draw a line from the task to a point in the month, rather than rewrite it. I use colored pens, stickers, highlighters—anything to liven it up. By the end of the month, it's a work of art. Abstract, but art all the same.

- Pockets and zipper pouches hold all kinds of handy things.

- My "to do" lists are built in.

- Journal pages, so I can do my journaling in those "on hold" or "in line" times that crop up during the day.

- Inspiring quotes, stories, and tips in a special "Words of Wisdom" section.
- Expense envelope and blank expense report forms.
- Stamps, letterhead, postcards, envelopes.
- A list of important dates like birthdays, anniversaries, holidays.
- Photographs.
- Gift certificates, so when I'm in that store I will have them with me.
- List of little piddly errands to run. I keep this up front, because I'd just love to lose it.
- Calculator/ruler combo.
- Ongoing projects have a separate section.
- Past accomplishments are kept in a section called "Get a Life." Again, it is uplifting to look back at a list of your past triumphs (and add to it, too)—it gives you a sense of perspective when you start thinking you aren't getting anywhere.
- Permanent reminders: water the plants, prep for Monday meeting, article due by the fifteenth of the month.

THINGS TO DO (TO CREATE) LISTS

There is no fun in having nothing to do. The fun is having a lot to do and not doing it.

—John Roper

Years ago, steel magnate Andrew Carnegie paid $64,000 to a consultant who gave him two ideas: 1) Write down what you have to do today; 2) Do the most important thing first. What's the most important task on your list? Highlight it, write it in red, circle it, then do it first!

While no product or tool will manage your time for you,

nothing has helped me more than a to do list. Don't fight it, try it.

Why a to do list? It eliminates that ugly feeling that you're forgetting something (which you probably are). It keeps you from having to depend entirely on memory (which wastes energy, creativity, and time). Rather than worrying about little details, you can focus on bigger, more important things. Even if you remember everything now (and if you think you do, it just means you've *completely* forgotten the things you've forgotten), you won't always.

You get older, your life gets more complicated, the lives of those around you get more complicated, and you gradually become aware that little things are starting to slip past you. "I know I was supposed to pick something up on the way home . . . what was it?" you'll ask yourself. And there's little Johnny (your son) sitting by the curb in a pouring rain waiting to be picked up by his daddy. If only his daddy used a to do list like all the other kids' daddies. . . .

Having a to do list (weekly, daily, whatever works for you) helps reduce the stress of trying to remember every little thing you must do, while eliminating the embarrassment you face when you forget something important. This, contrary to popular belief, actually increases creativity and flexibility by freeing up your mind to create and spend more time on the fun stuff.

Without a list, you can get caught up in trivial, useless, dead-end stuff. Before you know it, the day's over and you wonder, "Where did the time go? I didn't get anything worthwhile done today."

Keeping a to do list can be as simple as writing down a few things, highlighting key ones, then checking off or crossing out as you complete an item. You don't have to do everything on the list for your day to be a success. I figure if I get done a third of the stuff on my list, I've had a good day.

You're not supposed to be a slave to your list. It's just a tool. You don't even have to stick to it. Leave things undone if you can live with the consequences. But *choose* to leave them undone—don't skip things because they skipped your mind and try to rationalize it later. Let your to do list give you some focus and direction.

Let's look at the more traditional to do lists first, and I'll provide you with some tips to make them work. Then we'll explore some creative alternatives to the linear list.

- **Think about** whether it would be better for you to have a portable to do list or one mounted on your wall where you can see it easily.

- **Daily things to do list—items you must do today.** Keep this list short (some say no more than ten items). Some need the daily to do list for appointment times, expenses, errands, a long list of things to get done.

- **Don't forget to write in prep work** for things coming up next week/next month so they don't sneak up on you.

- **Use a checklist for repetitious tasks:** phone interview questions, the steps in a project, regular calls, work items, or appointments. You can preprint these, so you don't have to write them out each day.

- **Include fun stuff.** And make the less than fun stuff *look* more fun (draw a monster for a deadline, a throbbing tooth for a dentist appointment). My to do list has a cartoon of a little boy sticking his fingers in his ears and his tongue out. He has the attitude, so I don't have to.

- **Don't waste time rewriting it if your to do list is messy.** Just don't show it to anybody.

- **Keep it handy,** where you can refer to it easily (and often).

- **Be realistic about the number of things you can do in a day.** Put how long you think a task will take and stop after you hit eight (or twelve) hours to help tame the list.

- **Try a weekly list if a daily one is too much trouble.** When planning for the week, make sure to include both personal and professional areas of your life. A friend of mine had no place in his schedule for a simple oil change—and ended up paying major bucks to replace his engine block.

- **Weekly and monthly to do lists give a broader view,** which has advantages. I have to make phone calls today to get the material I need to work on next week so I can meet my deadline two weeks from today. The longer-range lists help you keep up with upcoming and ongoing projects.

- **Check it off.** Don't deprive yourself of the simple pleasure of crossing out or checking off as you complete each item. I know a guy who begins his daily to do list with "make to do list." This way, he claims, he gets a quick burst of accomplishment by checking it off (much like a shot of espresso to start the day. Wahoooo.)

- **There's no set way to make your list,** as long as you can read it and have a way to mark things off when they're done. Use no organization (write all over, every which way, no particular order), or organize by calls, errands, categories, appointments, area of town. Use one color for all the items relating to a particular client or project to make them hang together even if they're not written together.

- **If there's something you dislike doing that you have to do**—put it on your list. It's harder to avoid, and you get the extra boost from crossing it off when you're done.

- **If you only get partway done with an item,** make a note on the list about where you stopped or were going so you can pick up right where you left off without backtracking when you come back to it.

- **Use your to do list format for other kinds of lists**—shopping lists, checklists, travel lists, supply lists, birthday card lists, whatever.

- **Fit your to do list on one page and carry it with you.** Put calls, e-mail addresses, everything you need to for that day, on the list.

- **Do payoff things first** or what you enjoy doing. Getting a couple of things checked off right off the bat can put a positive spin on your whole day.

- **Do high-priority tasks at high-priority times.** A quick scan of your list can help you plan your day. "I have to call New York, and they're gone by two P.M. my time, so I need to make that call before lunch."

- **If you start feeling overwhelmed, do a little list surgery.** Ask yourself, "What's the worst thing that will happen if I don't do this task?" Depending on your answer, scratch it off your list entirely, put it on tomorrow's list, or find something else you can dump.

- **Write your goals at the top of the page.** Or you can try my assistant's version: She has a list of "I wants" on the top of her to do list. Some of them are silly ("I want to win the lottery"), some of them are potential rewards for completing her projects for the day ("I want to go out to dinner"), and some of them are long-term things she's working toward ("I want to get my son through college"). Whatever you call them, these goals or "I wants" can keep you focused, keep you working, because there's something concrete to work for.

- **Think twice about things before you put them on your list.** Is it worth writing down? Keep the crap off your list and out of your life.

- **Set off the one thing you *must* do today** either by writing it big or setting it off to the side. Or the top five things this week.

SOME CREATIVE APPROACHES TO LIST MAKING

Words make a difference. Instead of calling your list "Must do today" or "Things to do," try "Exciting challenges today," "Potential accomplishments," "Opportunities to shine," or "Things I choose to do today." Sounds more inviting now, doesn't it? Here are some more ideas:

- **Match your energy cycle to your daily to do list.** Draw a curved line with peaks and valleys. Put your creative or more difficult tasks along the peaks and your less creative or errand-type tasks in the valleys. Matching the degree of difficulty to your energy cycles works!

- **Make an anti–things to do list.** Things you do that are either a complete waste of time, you hate doing, should and could be done by someone else, or you can live without doing them. Post this on your wall and add to it whenever you feel you are in over your head or spinning your wheels. Just spelling these things out can actually give you the motivation to take care of/get rid of/delegate them.

- **Make it into a game.** This is one of my favorites. You compete against yourself. List all the things you have to do. Assign a point value to each one. (Keep it simple—ten, five, two points, depending on importance or degree of difficulty. I add in bonus points for exercising.) At the end of the day, total the points for the tasks you completed. Then total the points for the tasks you didn't finish. Which total is higher? At the beginning of the day, I write down some small prize I'll give myself if I "win." I have found that just by playing, you are winning.

- **Make a time line list.** (This comes from the book *Organizing for the Creative Person.*) On the left is the time you wake up, noon is near the middle, and whatever time you go to bed is on the far right. Turn the paper vertically. Your things to do, calls to make, appointments, and meetings are plotted along the timeline either with Post-it notes or by writing them in. Create a master time line, and make copies so you don't have to create a new one each day.

- **Make two lists,** one a right-brain list of all the fun stuff you *want* to do and the other a left-brain list of the things you *must* do.

- **Make it into a board game.** I play against my assistant. We each make a list of things to do, calls to make, and

TIME MANAGEMENT FOR THE *Creative* PERSON

so forth. We then have little colored pieces that move along a board we created. As you complete a task, you move your piece spaces depending on the difficulty (difficult, three spaces; tedious, two spaces; easy, one space). There are places on the board where you can draw a card; the cards give you fun things to do (half-hour break) or challenge you to do more (pick up one of other player's tasks). There are pitfalls along the way that force you to leap over them with a difficult task before you can move on. Create your own game to play with a co-worker. It makes the day go by faster, it's fun, and the winner not only gets bragging rights or a little prize, but you both get a lot more done!

- **Shuffle the deck.** Use a stack of index cards, one card for each item on your to do list, then shuffle them and do whatever comes up. Add in "wild cards" that allow you to take a break or do something fun for a while. Shuffle and draw throughout the day. Add in new cards as things come up. Or pin the cards to a wall or bulletin board in the order you think things should be done. (Write urgent things in red.) Move them around as your day changes. (I use different-colored cards for calls, meetings, and urgent items.)

- **Make it a cartoon strip.** Draw characters or symbols for each type of task. Meeting with your supervisor could be a mean-looking monster seated behind a desk. Lunch with Betty can be a picture of two people eating at an outdoor café. I draw fast, so this doesn't take as much time as it sounds, but you can buy inexpensive cartoons on CD and use those, too. Either way, it's pleasing to look at and makes unpleasant tasks seem, somehow, not so bad when they have a funny face.

- **Theme your list.** I like variety, so I have to do games themed for golf, football, baseball, and auto racing. As I complete a task, I move an imaginary golf ball along the green by drawing a line from the tee to the cup (it's a laminated picture of an actual golf course pinned to the wall). I move along in strokes drawn along the side of the picture based on how difficult the completed task was. It takes twenty strokes to finish the course. That's a good day. (There are hole-in-one tasks, too.) Or I move the football down the field, the little man around the bases, or the car along the track. Same principle, different picture.

- **Make three columns or circles on your paper,** "Must do no matter what," "Should do, but if I don't can do tomorrow," and "Things I want to do for me." Don't neglect that last column!

- **Mind Map your list.** Make a circle in the center of your page and write your things to do around the outside; put your most important thing to do in the middle. Then brainstorm everything involved with getting these things done, writing them on branches, and drawing lines to connect interconnected work. (This helps get away from the linear approach.)

- **Draw your things to do.** Heck, paint them if you want. Do them with crayons, colored markers, stickers. Make a pyramid and put your highest priority at the top and the least important tasks at the bottom.

TICKLER FILE

I have a simple philosophy. Fill what's empty.
Empty what's full. And scratch where it itches.
—Alice Roosevelt Longworth

A tickler file gives you a reminder of future events, follow-up, and an action file for the day. It's fast, functional, easy, manageable, and a huge time-saver. The disadvantage is that you have to sort through it every day. The advantage is it minimizes how much you have to sort through. Use it instead of or in conjunction with your calendar, to do list, and/or planner.

- **Use a one- to thirty-one-day expanding file** (I like one with no cover so you can just drop notes in).

- **A monthly version** (Jan.–Dec.) is needed for more long-range tickles.

- **Pull out what's in the file** and work on it or add to your to do list every day.

- **At the start of a new month,** pull out scraps and file by days.

- **Use neon paper** for important notes.

- **Keep your tickler file nearby** and at hand, portable.

- **Drop airline tickets,** party invitations and directions, birthday cards you already bought, doctor appointments with notes on what to ask, invoices due, bills to pay. A tickler file is best for items that have attachments. Otherwise a note on your calendar would do.

- **Use index cards** for notes to yourself; drop them in the appropriate slot.

- **For recurring deadlines** like a monthly newsletter, just move the reminder card from month to month.

- **For birthdays,** drop in an index card a day or two before to remind yourself to get a gift (anniversaries, too).

- **Great system for follow-up.** Drop a note in the tickler file for the day you expect a follow-up call, so you're aware of the problem if the call doesn't come in and you've reminded yourself of the subject if the call does come in.

CALENDARS

If you want something to happen, you have to make space for it.

—*David Campbell*

The calendar is the least amount of time management equipment you can get by with. It is the most basic, most indispensable, and often the cheapest tool you can use. If it keeps you from forgetting one anniversary, it was money well spent, no?

The following is a true story that I am sharing with you (despite great embarrassment to myself) to show that how you use your calendar is nearly as important as having one.

I was asked by a radio station to fill in for a vacationing talk show host. I agreed to be the guest host and secretly hoped they would offer me my own show in the future. As the producer was telling me what days I would be on, who my guests would be, and where the station was located, I wrote it down in my calendar along with his phone number. (So far, good.)

I had been a guest on the show once before and listened to it once in a while, so I didn't write down the start time of the program. The next day the producer called back to inform me that the show would be on an hour early because of the early start of a ball game. I made a mental note as he told me, *but never wrote it down on my calendar.* I contacted my first guest, and when he asked me what time to be there, I told him to be there thirty minutes before the old airtime! As I drove to that first show, I tuned in to the station and was surprised to hear not the ball game, but a tape of an old show with the regular host. I arrived at the station what I thought was thirty minutes early. Actually I was a half hour late. I have never been so embarrassed in my life.

So much for making a good impression on the producer and getting my own show. If I had only written down the time change in my calendar, this never would have happened.

To get the most from your calendar, try one or more of the following techniques:

- **Wall calendars with write-on and wipe off capabilities are the best.** Use stickers and Post-it notes with them, too.

- **Start blocking out time in pencil on your calendar** when you will work on a big project. You have to clear time for long-term stuff, or you'll never get to it.

- **Keep it on your desk** or on the wall in plain view.

- **Schedule exercise appointments;** block out the time.

- **Write library book due dates** on your calendar.

- **Write down *everything* you don't want to forget,** especially appointments.

- **Stick to only one calendar,** if possible. Use the one in your planner and keep it open on your desk. Use the same one for business and personal schedules. Some people have separate work, computer, planner, family, car, and briefcase calendars. That's at least four too many!

- **Use drawings, photos, stickers**—make it fun and make it visual, so a glance will tell you what you need to know.

- **Include address, phone, and directions when you note an appointment.** Get a calendar that has space to do this. Write in pencil.

- **Use stickers, colors, and highlighter** so you can quick scan your calendar for availability. Make appointments with yourself for networking, bookkeeping, or personal projects.

- **Two-page-spread calendars are the best,** giving you enough room to write.

- **Does it work?** If the calendar you're using doesn't work for you, get another kind and keep experimenting until you find one that has the features you need.

- **Don't schedule meetings in your peak hours.**

- **Schedule time to reflect,** recover, conceptualize.

- **Keep a family calendar in plain view,** color coding for each family member. Keep massive numbers of pens nearby or attach with a string. Note parties, vacations, open house, and so on. Don't forget to compare your own calendar with the family calendar.

- **Give kids their own calendars** to write down book report due dates, homework, science project deadlines, appointments, classes, parties, dates, events, and the like. Many schools encourage the use of kid planners.

- **Note birthdays or big events and projects in your calendar** with an advance warning to give you time to prepare, buy a present, pack, and so forth.

- **Build in white space for fun stuff.**

- **Coordinate your calendar** with those of your spouse, boss, co-workers, and clients. Just don't waste time copying information from one calendar to another. Photocopy your calendar if you need to.

- **Plan backward with big projects,** starting with the due date and working back to determine how much time you need to allot and when.

- **Desk pads are good if you have the room;** they're very useful for notes. The problem is they're not portable.

- **Create your own calendar on the computer** to match how you see the year. This also allows you to drop in symbols, pictures, colors. Print out a copy to take with you.

ADDRESS BOOKS

There are three kinds of address books these days: Rolodex, paper, and electronic. Most of us use some combination of these. If you have only an electronic one, it's a hassle when the computer's tied up printing or the system's down or the worst happens and you have a crash. So keep your most important numbers in your planner, too. If you don't have a planner, don't throw away your Rolodex in a fit of modernization. You *will* need a paper backup.

Some tips for managing your paper address book:

- **Divide it into business and personal numbers.** You could use white pages for personal and yellow pages for business, or buy two sets of address book pages, keeping business and personal address books separate but both of them in your planner.

- **Keep a backup copy of your address book.** If you use only one of the tips mentioned here, use this one.

- **Just staple business cards to your Rolodex cards** to save time. The Rolodex bummer is that it isn't portable, and it can get messy after a while.

- **Planner address books also get messy,** and reentering all your information when you get a new planner is a serious drag. As a consequence, more people are using computer address books. They can be a hassle to set up, but you only have to set them up once. Get one that lets you print out pages that fit your planner.

- **Keep a file for address updates,** to do while waiting for someone or on hold. I hire a college student to handle the big update jobs.

- **Clear plastic business card sheets in a binder don't work well** because it's hard to move them around without having to move the whole sheet, especially if they are alphabetized. By the time you have a couple of hundred cards, it can take half an hour to page through to the one card you need. If you take the cards out of the sheet often, they get dirty and the binder sheets tend to tear. A Rolodex is better.

8

· · · · ·

A SIGN OF THE TIMES

"Power" Tools

The three R's—reading, 'riting, and 'rithmetic—are no longer enough. We must add the three C's—computing, critical thinking, and a capacity for change.

—Fred Gluck
(That's actually four C's, but I still like his quote.)

 Has technology changed your life in the past couple of years? Well, you ain't seen nothin' yet. The best is yet to come.

Brains are in and brawn is out. Creative types are built to survive and thrive in this brave new world. In a culture that values a variety of interests, imagination, and creativity, people who can handle change, are open-minded, work well under pressure, and can go in several directions at once are needed, admired, and valued.

There's a lot of talk about the paperless society, but we aren't even a less-paper society yet. The average U.S. citizen consumes the equivalent of five times his or her own weight in paper each year. As for the prediction that we will eventually become a cashless society—for some of us, it's here now (we're broke).

As far as technology goes, as long as you realize that you can't always have the latest and greatest of everything made and that you don't have to master every kind of software on the market, as long as you aren't afraid to ask for help and get training, you'll do fine. Yes, computers are linear and logical. Yes, I'm going to recommend that you read the manual.

But electronic systems are becoming more and more a part of our daily life, and many of them are quite useful.

MICRORECORDERS

We do more talking progress than we do progressing.
—*Will Rogers*

Microrecorders are both portable and convenient if you don't have paper and pen (while working out) or your hands are tied up (driving). Keep it clipped onto the visor in your car, on your person, or in your briefcase. (You can do your work anywhere.)

Making notes on a microrecorder is neater than keeping notes on scraps of paper. They're great for remembering items for your grocery list, when you meet someone, when you get directions, and so on.

I keep one with me for those unexpected flashes of brilliance (not that often, but you never know when or where they'll strike). Or when I suddenly remember to do something important and don't want to forget it again. I also make notes to myself and play them back when I'm driving or jogging.

Microrecorders are very handy for interviewing people. Some writers use them because you can talk faster than you write, some because they're not intrusive the way a big recorder or a madly scribbling writer is. Either way, you get ideas or conversation down quickly and accurately. Later, you can go over the tapes and transcribe what you need. You can dictate letters, thank-you notes, and "things to do" lists that your secretary can type up. With the minirecorders that use standard-size cassette tapes, you can record a meeting, lecture, or class and listen to it again in your car. Use a tape-to-tape recorder and make a "best of" tape.

The advent of the more sophisticated digital recorders (no tape) has really revolutionized this tool. You can still dictate ideas, phone numbers, directions, and things to do, but now you can store them in separate voice folders marked

"Ideas" and "Phone Numbers" for easy retrieval. In addition, many have alarms that will go off at a set time—for instance, to remind you to "pick up dinner on the way home."

The controls have gotten easier to use, so you're not fumbling while driving, and some will put information like phone numbers on a small display. A few of the more expensive ones are voice activated, so all you have to do is state a name and that person's phone number will be displayed and vocalized.

For a lot less money than you would expect to pay, you can instantly record and then later locate important information, all while driving safely in your car, working out on the StairMaster, or mountain biking in the wilderness.

ELECTRONIC ADDRESS BOOKS

Technology is another word for tool. There was a time when nails were high-tech.

— Tom Clancy

Electronic address books are effective when they are icon based (visual and colorful), tied to a contact manager, allow key-word searches, offer warning bells, and carry items forward. The best ones can print out files as a Rolodex card or Day-Timer page or print your address list in a variety of categories, including zip code or area code. Some have enough room to add notes, most allow you to make changes easily, and they stay neat no matter how much you cram into them. Laptop address book software can even dial the phone for you.

However, it's easy to get in over your head with hardware and software that sound good but turn out to be expensive, limited, or hard to learn. It can be a bummer to have one more technology to stay on top of, research, learn, and upgrade.

Sometimes an electronic tool will give you an edge, simplify your life, and even be fun to use. Sometimes it's required by your work and you have to make the best of it.

PALMTOP PLANNERS AND PERSONAL DIGITAL ASSISTANTS (PDA'S)

The reason the computer can do work faster than a human is that it doesn't have to answer the phone.

—Unknown

The possible uses for your palmtop are many, some of them unique. They let you carry tons of information in your pocket or purse (e-mail addresses, client profiles, phone numbers, addresses, even files). They allow you to handle contacts/ time/data management all in one place with a single interface. Wireless technology allows you to e-mail or fax a map or a note to a friend. You can save your doodles, keep a scrapbook, jot down numbers and reminders, and store them for easy retrieval with one word: "Find." They even allow you to easily take notes and transfer them to your computer. You can drag and drop a name and address to an appointment calendar, print out key lists of addresses, code in alarms and reminders, dial the phone, color code things, and attach icons with your palmtop. It makes for less clutter on your desk and is very portable. Some let you use handwriting (once you teach it to read your scribbles) to take notes and print later, most will move uncompleted tasks to the next day automatically. Great for school, they work like a notebook but can recall things by category and retrieve information fast.

Then there's the bad news. Palmtops are expensive, you have to learn how to use them, they can break down and freeze up—and then you have no clue where you're supposed to be when. You have to enter information on a tiny keypad (or download from your computer), screens can be hard to read, and they won't always read your scribble. A palmtop is also easy to lose or steal—and once it's gone, you have to start all over.

Once you've decided to invest in a palmtop, think about the following:

- Make sure you have a way to back up data, and do it often.

- Look for ones that have add-on features and are expandable. (You may want to add city guides, and for-eign-language dictionaries.)
- Make sure you have the hardware needed to connect to your computer, and download or upload information.
- Find one that includes a calculator, thesaurus, dictionary, conversions, and other handy tools.

LAPTOPS

Looked in my laptop, what did I see? A flashing message said, Today therapy.

—*Jimmy Buffett*

I think it is apropos to mention Jimmy Buffett and laptops in the same breath. Mr. Margaritaville romanticizes in his songs about the kind of laid-back lifestyle that a laptop computer can theoretically help you realize. You can do your work just about anywhere with a laptop.

Picture this: You're at the beach (on a workday, or this isn't as much fun) with your bare feet propped up, a tropical drink beside you, your laptop resting on your knees, and palm trees all around. Out in the distance, you watch dolphins frolicking in the waves. You grin as you envision your co-workers stuck in their stuffy offices while you are cooled by the gentle breezes blowing through your hair. Ahhh, life is good.

Wake up! This is a dream. Although laptops do offer flexibility about where and when you do your work, the reality is, life isn't a beach quite yet. Your battery could die in the middle of the Peterman report and you lose an hour's worth of work. (You forgot to save because you were too distracted by the "scenery.") You have to squint so hard to see the screen, you get a headache.

Other possible pitfalls include spilling your sticky drink on your laptop, getting sand and suntan oil on the keys, or, worst case, someone swipes your computer when you go for a swim. Owning a laptop does not mean instant time savings.

I should be honest about this, though. Right now, as I write this chapter, I am at a coffeehouse that actually does look out onto the beach (if you crane your neck and there isn't any smog). I am semi-indoors, plugged into an outlet at the counter, and I always make sure I get a lid put on my drink.

Carry your laptop in a beat-up case that does *not* look like a computer case, and never let it out of your sight. Carry two fully charged batteries, an AC adapter, extension cords, tools to hook up to the modem, phone wires—and make sure it will turn on at the airport. Then a laptop has all the advantages of palmtops (although it's not as portable), plus many of the advantages of your home computer. If you do a lot of writing, however, that small keyboard is likely to get to you.

GIZMOS

There is more to life than increasing its speed.
—Mohandas Gandhi

A gizmo can save you time and/or energy, but it can just as easily become a burden. Buying these goodies and gadgets (and I have listed only a few here) can cost time in learning how to use them, maintaining them, and upgrading them. Some can be real time-savers:

- Headphones to listen to TV without disturbing your partner.

- A product that attaches to your phone to politely tell telemarketers where to go.

- A solar-powered lawn mower that automatically trims your yard all by itself (without any nagging, I might add). You don't even have to watch it (except that, at over $1,000, someone may steal it).

- Radios that have timers to record radio talk shows.

- Natural-light alarm clock that lets you wake up gently. Clock shines before the alarm so you wake up naturally, like waking up to the sun. Especially nice during those long Midwest winters.

- A handheld unit that will tell you where you are and give you directions to where you want to go. Can give you directions to restaurants, gas, hospitals, motels, and the like.

- A *big* clock in plain view from anywhere in your office.

- A digital watch with an alarm can be set to remind you it's time to go in the morning, get you out of meetings.

- A garage door opener means one less key to lose, fewer hassles.

- Keys with a beeper! (Clap your hands and there they are.)

9

· · · · ·

QUICK FIXES

Hundreds of Timesaving Tips You Can Use
Right out of the Box

How much time we lose in seeking our daily bread!
—Paul Gauguin

You don't really pay for things with money. You pay for them with time. And no matter what you do, you don't have enough time. That's just a fact of modern life. Which means you have to make choices.

If you had an extra hour to use every day, how would you use it? According to a recent survey, twenty-two million working moms with children under twelve would spend an extra hour

44%	with their children
28%	alone/personal time
15%	sleeping
10%	with spouse/mate
2%	working

(Survey by Bruskin-Goldring Research)

The following are specific tips to help you make the most of your time in nearly every area of your life. Many involve a trade-off between time and expense. Don't reject these automatically. Consider how valuable your time/happiness/personal life/creativity are to you. It's hard to put a dollar amount on such things. Ask yourself if an expenditure for a time/stress/effort–saving device will allow you to increase your productivity/earnings. Ask yourself if you care.

The other major category of time-savers involves combining two or more tasks. This adds no cost and often gives benefits above and beyond the time saved. Don't be limited by the suggestions offered in this category. Use them as a starting point. Be creative.

As always, don't expect every tip to work for you. Look for the ones that might, and implement them one at a time. Use the tip you've chosen every day for three weeks, until a habit is formed and you don't have to stop and think about it anymore. Then do the same thing for another time- or energy-saver.

Now for the tough part: Don't use that extra time (a minute here, a minute there, it adds up) to take on more. You'll end up in the same cluttered, overwhelmed spot you're in now. Consider the time you save a gift to yourself. You need it. You deserve it. The goals chapter at the end of the book will help you keep it.

To help keep your job under control:

- **Know your business.** Keep a page on every project you do, noting what it involved, any problems you had, how long it took, any expenses, and how much it paid. If it's an in-house project and you're paid a salary, note whether it took an extra night or weekend work to meet the deadline. Use these notes as a basis for planning or bidding future projects.

- **Keep your door closed.** An open door is an invitation to interruption.

- **Don't have a visitor's chair in your office**—or if you do, pile it up with papers. People popping into your office won't be tempted to stay as long if they're forced to stand.

- **Make your phone calls all together at one time of day.** Put on the answering machine/voice mail for the rest of the time.

- **Use a weekly planner.** Don't try to stick yourself into hourly pegs.

- **Set aside ten minutes first thing each morning** to look at your day and see what you need to get done. Then allow twenty minutes on Friday afternoon to get an overview.

- **Flexibility is not likely your problem.** Allow time for the unexpected, the surprise addendum to your project, for polishing and making it pretty.

- **Go through your mail next to your trash basket.** Keep catalogs and reports in the bathroom, where you can read them at your leisure.

- **If you feel yourself getting frenzied,** *stop.* Give yourself five minutes of quiet time. Close your eyes. Stretch. Walk around the block. It'll pay off in productiveness later.

- **Most often,** *you're* **the one who puts you in a time crunch**—either through procrastinating, lack of planning, an overoptimistic estimate of the time required to complete a task, or the habit of taking on more than one person can properly handle. Take a look at your job—whose expectations are you trying to live up to? How realistic are they? How can you bring them into line with reality?

- **Delegate detail work wherever possible.** Use secretaries, interns, co-workers, outside services.

- **Stop complaining.** It's amazing how much time you'll save.

- **Focus on what you can control.**

● ●

Fun Facts

Just so you know, studies show that more than half of all telecommuters work late at night, keep unconventional hours, and occasionally work weekends. On the flip side (although the strange hours sound fine to me) is the amount of money they save by staying home—up to $200 a month on food, over $100 a month on gas, parking, and auto insurance, and $100 a month on clothes.

● ●

WORKING AT HOME

The only problem with working at home is that you're always at work.

—*Beth Hagman*

Cartoonist Scott Adams, who created *Dilbert,* was fired from a corporate job and now works at home. He's got a pool table in his office, watches TV while he works, doesn't bother to dress—at all—and annoys his cats for a creative break. He likes working at home because he has control of his schedule, the commute is twenty seconds, and he likes the isolation. The main drawback is that he tends to work nonstop, sending e-mail at midnight and sleeping whenever.

If you're working at home, you're already saving time by not having to commute. Most people don't dress as formally for a home office as a corporate one, and that saves time, too. The following are some more ways to carve a few extra minutes out of your day:

- **Meet clients outside your home office.** It gets you out, keeps you from being isolated. Combine trips to see clients with errands.

- **Set aside a day for meetings** and have two or three, with some cushion time between in case they run long (they will). You're not going to get anything done that day anyhow, so you might as well make as many contacts as possible.

- **Set up a storage area** and buy office supplies in bulk, preferably by mail or through a store that delivers.

- **Take breaks.** Set your computer to chime or an alarm clock to ring every couple of hours to remind you to get up, move around, stretch. This may seem like an expenditure of time instead of a savings, but you'll last longer if you do it. Burnout is a huge time-waster.

- **Buy prefab forms** or computer software to simplify invoicing, tracking expenses, handling taxes, and the like.

- **Take care of your banking/invoicing/inventory at a regular time each week.** It can take days to unsnarl an account, only minutes to keep it from snarling in the first place.

- **Hire a part-time assistant,** bookkeeper, intern, or housekeeper to take care of routine tasks you don't have time to handle or the skills to handle properly.

- **Hire help on a contract basis**—saves hours of tax work and horrendous amounts of tax liability over having an employee. There are very specific legal definitions to deal with here, however, so be careful. Check with your accountant or lawyer.

- **Put the laundry in the machine** or start/empty the dishwasher while you're on a break. But don't let household chores interfere or distract you from your work.

HOME IS WHERE THE HEART IS (THE TV, TOO)

My mother waited patiently by the door with three coats in her arms as my two younger brothers and I stood by her side. We were going to Grandma's house. When my dad came down the stairs, he asked, "Why are you just standing there?" As she handed him the coats, she said, "This time, *you* put on the children's coats, and I'll honk the horn."

Children emulate their parents' behavior when they grow up. You may say, "I'll never be like my mom," but then one day it happens. "I've become my mother, aaauuughhhh!"

When it comes to time management (or mismanagement), much of what we know and do stems from watching how our parents did it. Maybe it's time to find some other ways.

CHILDREN

Remember, no matter how bad a child is, they're still good for an exemption on your income tax return.
—*Unknown*

Don't be afraid to involve your children in your campaign to get a life. They can actually help! Try these tips on for size:

- **Take your children shopping with you.** It can be educational (for them) and quality time (for you). Use the time together to talk and bond.

- **Combine folding the laundry with watching them play.** Or read them a story while they take a bath. Or make a game out of picking up toys.

- **Teach them how to do more things for themselves** with patience and examples and a simplified approach. Make up an index card with the proper arrangement of silverware so they can set the table. Set out their outfits the night before school, and teach them about color coordinating. Show them how to clean their own rooms by simplifying the process (scoop and stash) with bins for their toys or sleeping bags that can be rolled up rather than a blanket to fold.

- **Do a reality check every once in a while.** If your ten-year-old needs a planner to keep up with all her extra-curricular activities, you're both overdoing. Cut back.

- **Make doing chores fun by doing them together.** My best friend's mom declared Saturday morning house-cleaning time. Everyone turned to, all with jobs appropriate for their age, and worked for two hours while she played John Philip Souza marches on the stereo.

Even I got into the act and helped out. In the end, the house was clean and we felt both energized and virtuous. Even very small children can participate, learning the benefits of teamwork. It's a great way to get things done while spending time together.

- **Take preventive measures.** A clean house can sometimes be as simple as keeping the dirt out. Have your children get in the habit of leaving their dirty shoes outside.

- **Stagger bathroom times** in the morning to avoid a logjam. (No pun intended.) The simplest way to do this is to get everybody up at fifteen-minute intervals (you first).

- **Start a family message center** with a calendar for the kids to write their appointments on (baseball games, recitals, open house at their school, and so on). If there's already something scheduled for that day or time, deal with it early on. You'll avoid stress and a lot of running around if there aren't last-minute scheduling conflicts.

PET TRICKS

The greatest pleasure of a dog is that you may make a fool of yourself with him and, not only will he not scold you, but he'll make a fool of himself, too.

—Samuel Butler

Like other family members, pets need attention, affection, cleaning up after, and feeding. Some pets are more work than others. A dog will come when he's called, a cat will take a message and get back to you. Regardless of the type of pet, they serve an important purpose. They can reduce worries, cheer you up, be your best friend, help teach children responsibility—and you can't beat that unconditional love. The downside, if there is one, is that pets can be time-consuming. Here are some ideas to help ease some of the burden.

- **Choose a pet that requires less of your time,** if that's a concern. A carpenter friend of mine gets enough satisfaction from a bird feeder outside his shop window.

- **Preventive care can save time down the road.** Make sure your pet has all the shots he needs to keep healthy.

- **Train your dog to walk at a good pace** (without stopping to sniff at or pee on every tree and fire hydrant). Then make his daily walk part of your exercise routine.

- **Brush your dog or cat while watching your favorite TV show,** returning phone calls, or spending personal time with your children, friends, or significant other.

- **Use an automatic feeder**/water bowl that requires only weekly fill-ups.

- **Buy pet food in bulk**—saves money and trips to the store.

- **Have a professional trainer housetrain your dog** and teach him manners.

PLANTS

A house plant will never talk back to you, and you don't have to walk a begonia.

—*Lynn Rapp*

Caring for any living thing can be relaxing, rewarding, and regenerating—plants included. They also help oxygenate your atmosphere. More oxygen in the air means more oxygen in your blood, more oxygen to your brain, and happy thoughts.

Silk plants, of course, don't provide the same kind of pleasure as real plants, but they require less effort (just an occasional dusting).

Here are some suggestions and time tips for maintaining healthy houseplants (the real kind):

- **Water, weed and feed at the same time** every day/week.

- **Keep all your plant stuff in one easy-to-reach place.**

- **Choose plants that are easy to grow** and maintain (ones that don't drop a lot of leaves or require daily watering).

- **Keep a water bottle handy** (a good idea if you're training pets, too).

- **Buy tools, seeds, and other plant supplies by mail.**

HOUSEWORK

I hate housework! You make the beds, you do the dishes, and six months later you have to start all over again.

— *Joan Rivers*

Women tend to take household chores personally. They feel people judge them on the cleanliness and appeal of their homes—and to some extent, that's true. Men don't feel such social pressure, and they're less likely to notice or care about dirt or mess. They tend to subscribe to the little elves theory as described in the book *More Time for Sex* by Harriet Schechter. They believe little elves fold the laundry, put away the dishes, and scrub the toilet. As my wife once clearly pointed out, however, *there are no elves!*

Anna Quindlen notes that when men do the dishes, it's called *helping*. When women do the dishes, it's called *life*. But according to a study by the University of Washington, husbands who share household chores with their wives are emotionally and physically healthier than those who don't. So here are some timesaving tips (for both sexes) on making housework less of a burden:

- **Put it in a hat.** In *I Hate Housework*, Peg Bracken suggests writing the worst jobs on slips of paper (my worst is taking out the recycling) plus some fun stuff (my favorite is going to the movies) in a three-to-one fun-stuff-to-chores ratio, then draw a couple times a week. (This works!)

- **Think about it.** Paula Jhung, author of *How to Avoid Housework,* has a system to make the bed while you're still in it and then slipping out. Unfortunately it doesn't work for changing the sheets.

- **Let it go.** If you have something more important or meaningful to do or you just don't feel like it, forget about the housework. Will it matter in five years that you didn't clean the grout on your counter? Not likely. The only housework that's really essential is the stuff that'll make you sick if you don't do it, like washing dishes or cleaning the catbox; and the stuff that'll break your bank if you avoid it too long, like cooking meals.

- **Do laundry less often** by wearing things twice. I know this sounds gross, but as long as you have clean underwear, you don't really have to wash those jeans after every wearing.

- **Switch to low-maintenance landscaping,** easy-to-clean surfaces, and plastic covers for high traffic areas.

- **Get a larger trashcan!** (My favorite timesaving tip, because I hate to take out the trash almost as much as I hate broccoli.)

- **Do a little at a time.** Do one chore each day before work. By the weekend they're all done and you're freeeeeeeeeee.

- **Hire a housekeeper** (my wife's favorite timesaving tip). It's well worth the money in time, stress, and marital harmony.

TOO MANY COOKS

The best way to clean a frying pan that has burned food cemented to the bottom is to let it soak in soapy water for several days and then, when nobody is looking, throw it in the garbage.

—Dave Barry

Biggest time-wasters in the kitchen in a survey for Tupperware U.S., Inc.

1. Lack of organization 55%
2. Routine chores (dishes, clean stove) 36%
3. Preparing food (chopping, peeling) 33%
4. Lack of correct utensils 24%

Ordering Chinese takeout does away with all the above time-wasters (assuming you have chopsticks). I know people whose first four speed-dial numbers are for pizza delivery—very efficient, no dishes or silverware needed. Most of us do use the kitchen at least occasionally, however, and there are several timesaving tips that might come in handy:

- **Keep take-out menus** from favorite restaurants in your home, office, and car. It saves time to call in your order and then go pick it up.

- **Ready-made salads** with precut veggies, boneless chicken breasts, canned sauces, Minute rice, and similar products all save time. Frozen dinners have come a long way from the old Salisbury steak/Tater Tots/apple pie days. (I still have nightmares about those things.) Combine a frozen entrée with fresh vegetables or a salad for a dinner that's both fast and fairly healthy.

- **Make enough for two meals** when you do cook, and freeze the second meal for next week. Or freeze several small portions for quick meals anytime.

- **Buy easy-to-clean pots and pans**, floor coverings, oven, and so on.

- **Fix one-pot meals** like stir-fry, chili, pot roast, or stews.

- **Use the crock pot** so dinner's ready when you get home.

- **Simplify cleanup, or get help.** A friend always cooks lasagna the night before the housekeeper comes—it makes a mess, but she can leave it overnight without a twinge of guilt.

- **Wash as you cook,** so the mess doesn't get out of hand. (Don't you hate to come back to the kitchen later after everything has adhered to surfaces as if bound with superglue?)

- **Peel food over the trashcan** or garbage disposal so it goes right in, saving a step. This is great if you compost.

- **Keep a list of ingredients** for your favorite dishes and take it with you to the grocery store on your way home from work. It's a good idea to keep an ongoing grocery list, too, writing in staple items as you run out of them.

- **Always have key ingredients** on hand for quickie meals (pasta and sauce, frozen chicken breasts, cans of soup, and so on).

- **Set up the coffeemaker** the night before and put it on a timer.

- **Minimize.** Harriet Schechter of The Miracle Worker Organizing Service boasts that she only saves recipes that use five or less ingredients.

- **Use paper plates and cups,** especially for the kids.

- **Leave cooking utensils out** and convenient, hanging in plain view.

ERRANDS

In the movie *Multiplicity,* Michael Keaton finds himself so overwhelmed with things to do that he decides to duplicate himself (three times) with the help of a scientist. His clones manage to give him some breathing room but cause other problems.

You don't have to duplicate yourself (no matter how much you'd like to) to get one of the biggest time-killing, energy-draining, pain-in-the-neck challenges under control. Here are some suggestions on how to handle errands without the hassles:

- **Do as much as possible in one trip,** once or twice a week.

- **Use places that pick up and deliver** (like dry cleaners or a freezer food service).

- **Shop in a store or shopping center** where you can consolidate as many of your errands as possible. Cleaners, photos, stamps, takeout food, prescriptions, ATM, postal services, and groceries can often be handled all in one stop.

- **I keep things in my trunk that I need to drop off** but don't want to make a special trip for. For instance, I stash things I want to give to my parents in my trunk, and when I'm in the neighborhood I stop by. Everything is already with me, which saves another trip.

- **Call the store before going to buy a hard-to-get item** to make sure it's in stock before making the trip. Call before going to pick up a special order or repair. Always call the airline to check on flight status before going on a trip or picking someone up.

- **Try to schedule appointments** back to back or all in the same day. With both kids at the dentist at the same time, you can go to a bookstore. This doesn't work if you're chronically late—or if your dentist is.

- **Keep a running list of errands** with you. Add and cross off as you go. The crossing-off part feels great.

- **Establish a drop zone** near the door for video returns, repairs, and items that need to be dropped off somewhere.

- **Delegate.** Who says *you* have to do it?

Prepared and Spared

Do you have spares of the following items?

Band-Aids, diapers, vacuum bag, cash, checks, stamps, keys, disks, VCR tapes, pens and pencils, art supplies, paper, flashlight, batteries, film, glasses, shoelaces, light bulbs, trash bags, toilet paper, candles, feminine hygiene products. You definitely don't want to run out of feminine-type stuff. Whenever I have to buy those damn things for my wife, the checker yells, "Price check on Tampons!"

• •

LOW MAINTENANCE

"I'll never, ever cut my hair." That's what I said to my parents when I was younger, in my rebellious musician days. Well, never say "never." I later discovered how much easier it was to manage short hair.

Here are some helpful timesaving tips for both men and women—regardless of the length of your hair. Granted, it can take longer for women to get ready (men *generally* don't have to shave their legs or have their bikini lines waxed), but some general ideas can help both get out the door faster:

- **Simplify your system for getting ready.** If you have to go to another room to finish putting on your makeup, you may be distracted by the TV or the kids or the dog on your way.

- **Get an easy-care haircut.**

- **I keep a toothbrush in every bathroom in the house.** I brush more often, because it's easier. I don't even want to think about how much dentist time I save.

- **Combine things:** floss while letting your conditioner set, or use an electric razor while commuting to work.

- **A more powerful blow dryer** can be a big time-saver.

TIME MANAGEMENT FOR THE *Creative* PERSON

- **Do your own nails** while you're watching TV or talking with a friend or spouse. Better yet, share nail duty with your friend while you spend quality time together.

- **Shower the night before.** Save baths for lazy, romantic weekends.

QUICK QUIZ

What do you think is the average length of a shower in the United States?

Answer: 12.2 minutes, according to a recent survey. (For women between the ages of eighteen and twenty-four, an average shower lasts 16.4 minutes. What are they *doing* in there?)

DRESS FOR SUCCESS

True elegance consists not in having a closet bursting with clothes, but rather in having a few well-chosen numbers in which one feels totally at ease.

—*Coco Chanel*

Einstein wore the same color suit every day. Calvin Klein switches off between jeans and a blue blazer and khakis and a blue shirt. For some people, this is a good idea—fewer decisions to make, less time spent shopping, less money spent because fewer clothes are needed when everything matches everything else. Find the colors and cuts you look best in and stick with them.

Taken to the extreme, this method is unrealistic and boring. But simply limiting your color scheme can be a big time-saver.

- **Lay clothes out the night before** (with accessories) so you notice wrinkles, stains, tears, and missing buttons before it becomes a crisis. It can take three times as long to decide what to wear in the morning.

- **Buy low-maintenance clothing.** Clothes that don't stain or wrinkle easily, and those that don't need to be dry-cleaned or ironed, will save time and money.

- **Shop by catalog.** Mail order is a great time-saver.

- **A personal shopper is convenient.** They learn your likes and dislikes as well as your sizes and can call you when something appropriate comes in. Saves you all that fruitless, frustrating shopping time. This is good only for those who don't use shopping time as social, inspirational, fun, or "for myself" time.

- **Use fewer accessories.** Go for quality, not quantity. (My wife tells me diamonds go with everything.)

- **Use solid basic colors for separates, shoes, and handbags**—they're easier to match than patterns and prints.

- **Avoid having to iron wrinkled garments** by washing smaller loads and putting them on a hanger right out of the dryer.

- **Buy underwear, socks, or hosiery in bulk** and do laundry less often.

- **Tie ribbons on the handles of the washer and dryer** you're using at the Laundromat for quick and easy identification.

- **Buy your own washer/dryer.** Then you can do your laundry while you're cooking dinner, reading, watching TV, or cleaning house. Whenever you can do two things at once, you come out ahead. This doesn't work for people who use the Laundromat as a meeting place or a quiet getaway.

- **Have your laundry done for you.** It may be worth the money.

CIRCLE OF FRIENDS

I have lost friends, some by death, others by sheer inability to cross the street.

—*Virginia Woolf*

Creative people can be somewhat self-involved—loners who are maybe a little careless when it comes to their friends. A recent survey revealed that people in the 1990s have cut back on the time they spend with friends.

I recently saw a car that looked a lot like one belonging to an acquaintance of mine. As I walked toward it, I saw him reach down as if to pick something up—only he never came back up. He was hiding from me. I could have pretended not to see him and moved on, but that's no fun. Instead I knocked on his window. He shot up from a fetal position on the floor.

"Uh, hi, Lee," he muttered.

"What were you doing down there?" I asked. "Hiding?"

"Well, yeah, I'm in the middle of writing a screenplay and I didn't want to talk to anyone. I'm kinda in character."

I forgave him. What can I say?

I value friendship above almost all else and find it to be rewarding in many ways. It really doesn't take that much effort. You don't have to be constantly in each other's company like TV's "friends" Ross, Rachel, Chandler, Joey, Monica, and Phoebe. Just make a little time to maintain close friendships with positive people.

DO THINGS TOGETHER. Have your hair cut side by side, bake together, run errands together, get your nails done together, work out, garden, fix your car, share a hobby, take a class, see a play or movie, volunteer together, have your kids play together, learn a new skill—together.

FAX A FRIEND A FUNNY CARTOON. Send a card, clip an article, forward a good recipe, e-mail a joke. All these things show that you are thinking about them but take very little time. I take my address book with me when I'm on the road doing seminars and send postcards to friends and acquaintances I haven't talked to in a while.

REMEMBER THEIR BIRTHDAYS AND SPECIAL OCCASIONS. Mail a card, send flowers, or leave a funny (singing) message on their machine.

TRUE LOVE

It's worth the time to make your romantic relationships special—nothing is so inspiring to the creative spirit. If you're smart, though, you can get the most out of a romance without spending all your time on it. Try some of these tips:

- **Hang a sign** that says "I love you" where your lover will see it in passing.

- **Dedicate a song** on the radio.

- **Be good Samaritans together.** Take coffee and blankets to the homeless, volunteer to serve at a soup kitchen, or make a Big Brother/Big Sister commitment.

- **Surprise your love** by arriving in a limo to whisk him or her off for lunch. Then drive through the local burger stand and eat in the car.

- **Give them your undivided attention** when you're with them. That way, they won't mind so much when you're not.

- **Call when you know they won't be home** and leave a special message on their machine. You don't get involved in a lengthy conversation, but they know you care.

- **Leave a flower on their car.** Or hide Post-it love notes all over the house.

- **Write "I love you"** in the dust on the dining room table (actually, this one wasn't particularly popular with my wife, who took it as a comment on her housekeeping).

- **Take lessons together.**

- **Camp out in the backyard.** No travel time—all fun time.

- **Create your own drive-in.** Put the TV and VCR in the garage. Park your car and turn off the engine (please).

Bring your own popcorn, and it's just like a real drive-in (but much more private, and you have a remote control).

- **Be their slave for a day.** If you're like my wife and me, that means the house gets cleaned, too.

- **Spend a weekend being a tourist in your own town—** quicker, cheaper, and less stressful than going away, and often more entertaining.

THE RELUCTANT HOST

Like migrating geese, guests start flying in when the weather warms. It's illegal to shoot them and impolite to shoo them away, so we have to know how to handle them without ruffling their feathers.

—*Paula Jhung*

Some may refer to them as freeloaders, home wreckers, or Katos, but houseguests may just be your best friend, mother, or brother. Sure, they take up your time and space and eat your food and wear on your patience, but I have some solutions to make sure their stay is both short and sweet.

Your guests don't mean to be a pain. And they won't be, if you just give them a little direction (and a few subtle hints).

- **Get rid of any spare rooms.** This act alone can eliminate unwanted houseguests altogether and at the same time give you a home office, quiet space/library, sewing/art room, or extra storage.

- **Dedicate one full day to your guests,** then let them do their own thing.

- **Make your guests self-sufficient** by providing them with an easy-to-use alarm, their own towels in a different color, their own soap, and so on. Have novels of all kinds available for guests to read, rent movies for them, introduce them to your friends.

- **Rather than cook, dine out**—and let your guests pay.
- **If they offer to help clean, *let them*.**
- **Think twice** before you blurt out, "Hotel, schmotel, stay with us."
- **Provide maps, books, bus schedules, tour information.** Then set a time and place to meet toward the end of the day.

PARTY HEARTY

The other aspect of entertaining is the fine art of throwing a party, which has been compared to having a baby—its conception is more fun than its completion, and once you've begun it's almost impossible to stop.

After one party, a friend of mine told his wife, "Clean up this? Can't we just sell the house?"

There are easier ways to handle hosting duties (the easiest being to give the job to a hostess). Seriously, the following can help you put together, enjoy, and clean up a party with as little time trauma as possible:

- **Combine and conquer.** Stephanie Shur, a professional organizer, says to throw a simple once-a-year bash and invite all your friends rather than entertain a few friends a month. This saves both time and money.

- **Clean the bathroom first.** If you have time to clean only one area, this is it. Nobody should have to see your dirty toilet.

- **After-party cleaning is more important than before.** Only early arrivals will notice any mess (steer them straight to the bar).

- **Keep a well-stocked bar** (see foregoing).

- **Mail an invitation to yourself** to be sure they arrive okay and how long they take to get there. Or e-mail your invitations. It's faster, cheaper, and hipper.

- **On the invitations, be sure to include all pertinent information,** including appropriate attire, special parking instructions, and a detailed map to the party. This saves time having to tell each guest over the phone.

- **Get help.** Co-op a party with a friend, hire a caterer, or enlist the help of your kids.

- **Make a guest list, shopping list, and errand list** on index cards or a small pad that you can carry with you and add to when an idea strikes.

- **Have a theme.** It spices up almost any affair and helps limit your options. Once you've made the theme choice, everything else falls into place.

REALLY HAPPY HOLIDAYS

I never believed in Santa Claus because I knew no white dude would come into my neighborhood after dark.

—Dick Gregory

Holidays can be a joy. They can also be a burden. To make the most of your time with family and friends and still manage to get your work done, simplify your holiday routine as much as possible. Sometimes that means rethinking traditions that no longer work for you. It can even mean sacrificing your reputation for having the most beautifully wrapped gift package under the tree. Then again, you can develop a new reputation for having the biggest smile in the room.

- **Everything doesn't have to be made from scratch,** or even made at all. Have holiday meals catered. Or pot luck—it's more fun for everyone.

- **Do the Tom Sawyer thing.** Make holiday meals and baking and candy making into family affairs where everybody sings while they work together and your mate or housekeeper does the cleanup.

- **Hire a cleaning team** to come in and make the house sparkle before the holidays.
- **Get away from anxiety** with a trip during or just before the holidays. (Hawaii is always nice this time of the year.)
- **Have family get-togethers** at a different house each year, to spread the stress around.
- **Draw names so everyone has to get only one gift.** This saves time and money. Just don't get competitive about giving the best gift each year.
- **Buy your holiday cards at the after Christmas sales** so you have them ready to send early in December. My friend doesn't have time to send cards before the holidays, but she doesn't stress. She just sends Happy New Year cards instead and spends New Year's Day writing notes and addressing envelopes while she watches the parades. It's a pleasant start to the year, remembering friends and family.
- **Just sign the holiday card.** Don't feel you have to send a letter with each one. Or put together a single long note—be humble now, no bragging—and include it with everybody's card.
- **Keep the holiday spirit throughout the year.** When you see a perfect gift for someone, buy it and cross that person off your list.
- **Shop through catalogs.** Once you buy out of a catalog, you'll get tons of them for all kinds of things. You may never have to leave your house again.

FOOD FOR THOUGHT

*I don't even know how this word came into being:
Aerobics. I guess gym instructors got together and
said, "If we're going to charge $10/hr., we can't call
it Jumping Up and Down."*

—*Rita Rudner*

Some people would rather have their jaws wired shut or their stomachs stapled than exercise. Exercise and fitness don't have to take much time, and they certainly don't have to be drudgery. The positives that come from being fit include increased self-esteem and more energy—and more energy translates into more time.

Most of us use lack of time as an excuse for not doing what we should. You're in a rush and grab a quick but unhealthful snack or meal. You drink coffee and soda for the caffeine instead of water. You put off exercise until later in the day, and then you never get around to it.

I'm speaking from experience. All my life I've been very athletic. After I got married (my wife's a good cook) and started spending more and more time on the road (the two things have nothing to do with each other), I put on weight—a lot of weight. I ballooned to an unhealthy size, according to my doctor. But it wasn't until none of my clothes fit anymore and I felt uncomfortable when I was *naked* that I decided to do something about it. I lost thirty-five pounds and have kept them off. The surprising thing is that it takes very little effort to maintain this weight, because fitness has become a way of life again.

Here are some simple tips for better health that require very little in the way of time and, in many cases, can actually save you time.

- **Don't skip breakfast to save time.** This doesn't help you lose weight and can leave you listless during the mid-morning hours, which should be the most productive of your day.

- **Fast food can be healthy.** Choose lower-fat/lower-calorie quick foods like rice bowls with meat and vegetables or energy bars—some of them actually taste good.

- **Go ahead and nosh.** Eat small meals, and eat often. This helps keep your energy level up and your digestive system happy.

- **Head for the Hunan.** Hot, spicy food increases your metabolism by 25 percent.

- **Don't use food as a reward.** If you're really smart, you'll use exercise itself as a reward—a trip to the beach/lake/mall for a long walk or run, a half day off for a bicycle ride, a weekly aerobic kaffeeklatsch, a swim followed by a steambath or sauna.

- **Invest in your own happiness.** The happier/busier you are, the less you crave food.

- **Vary your exercise routine.** Keep it interesting. Use your creativity.

- **Everything is exercise.** One woman I read about wears her jogging suit when she has her nails done, jogs while they dry, then drives home.

- **Invest in fitness equipment and a trainer.** Working out at home saves you the time spent going to the gym. You get a more concentrated workout, and the trainer will keep you on track toward your fitness goals.

- **Do abdominal exercises between weight-lifting sets.** It helps keep up your heart rate and you don't have to do them later.

- **Do everyday things more actively:** housework, walking to the mailbox, watching TV, sex, whatever. Move around, move faster, use more of your muscles.

- **Always have a set of workout wear with you.** Then take advantage of any opportunity that arises.

- **Not stretching is *not* a time-saver** (before and after exercise).

- **Ride your bike to work** if the weather is nice or it's casual day. Take stairs, walk places, park a block or two away from where you're going.

- **Ride your exercise bike** or use the treadmill while you read the paper or watch the morning news show.

- **Take a quick walk around the building** during your break time and after lunch. Ten minutes of exercise three times a day can be as effective as thirty minutes of exercising once a day.

- **Wash your hands to prevent illness** (rubbing and rinsing is the key). Getting sick is a totally unnecessary time-waster.

- **Get your shots.** A vaccination that prevents you from catching this year's flu can save you a week of being laid up in bed.

- **Alcohol, smoking, and drugs** rob you of your time, health, and creativity. Singer/songwriter David Crosby had to have a liver transplant after years of drug and alcohol abuse. "While I was an addict, I didn't write anything. I didn't have the attention span or the will," he admitted.

- **Get a physical.** Having a doctor tell you that you're in good health can be a load off your mind and keep you from wasting time looking for symptoms. Many health insurance policies these days cover physicals under preventive medicine.

- **Poor mental health** is another thing that can rob a person of creative juices. Many talented and creative individuals have fought depression. F. Scott Fitzgerald once said, "Every act of life, from the morning toothbrush to the friend at dinner, became an effort. I hated the night when I couldn't sleep and I hated the day because it went toward night." Get help.

IT'S NOT HARD TO FIND HELP

If you hate to do something, chances are you won't. At the very least, you'll procrastinate until it goes away or ends up costing you more in time, money, and effort. What's the solution? Get help.

My biggest "hate to do it" thing is learning a new software program. I find it much easier to hire someone to show me how it works (while getting a project done) than to read the manual or learn by trial and error. I don't consider this a weakness. It's smart to do what you do best and let others take care of the other stuff.

Here are some other areas where it pays to hire someone else to do it for you:

- **If you need to paint or move, have a party.** You order the pizza and supply the sodas or beer, and the job turns into fun. It gets done quickly, and you get to spend time with friends, too.

- **Keep phone numbers of your "team"** of helpers at your fingertips, with backups in case they're already booked or busy.

- **Hire a regular housecleaner**—you don't just save chore time. When your house is clean, you don't waste time hunting for what you need in the clutter. And you don't waste energy yelling at everybody else to clean up after themselves.

- **Get high school or college kids** (or your own kids) to help for cheap.

- **Pet watchers and walkers** can be time-savers; so can gardeners, fitness trainers, and laundry services.

- **Barter.** Create a newsletter for your accountant; in exchange, he does your taxes.

- **Hire a consultant** to help you work out your finances, your storage needs, your marketing plan. Getting organized at the start makes things easier throughout a project. If you're not good at organizing, hire someone who is.

BOOB TUBE

TV does not exist to entertain you, it exists to sell you things.

—*Gene Roddenberry*

The average American spends twelve years watching TV. (We spent two years on the O. J. trial alone!) At an average of sixteen hundred hours of TV a year, that equals continuous watching from July Fourth to Labor Day.

In 1980 just over 1 percent of households had a VCR; in 1994 79 percent did. I see that as a positive sign, actually. Now you can live your life on your own time schedule and tape your favorite shows to watch later, without the commercials, in a quarter of the time.

- **Have a TV night with friends** to watch your favorite shows or *Monday Night Football*. According to ABC, seventeen million households watch *Monday Night Football*.

- **Cut back on TV.** It's the single thing you can do to give you more time. Four hours per day equals *ten years* of your life.

- **Use the TV as a message center.** A friend of my wife's told us she tapes notes to the TV for her husband to be sure he sees them. (My wife tapes notes to the computer.)

- **Limit yourself to a single news hour** or newspaper you trust.

- **Tape shows/sporting events.** If you haven't gotten around to watching them in a week, tape over them.

- **Make TV harder to get to** (closing doors) or out of the way (in a den or bedroom) so you're not tempted to watch it as often.

- **Circle shows to watch in *TV Guide*.** This keeps you from channel surfing when there's nothing on you really want to see.

- **Rent movies or subscribe to a movie channel**—saving time and money over going to the theater.

- **Turn off the TV.**

● ●

Things You Can Do While Watching TV

Mend or sew, clip coupons or sort old ones, write letters, file nails, polish shoes, work out (my favorite team had a bad year, and the frustration fueled some great workouts).

● ●

TIME WAITS FOR NO ONE

If it weren't for Laundromats, half the letters in the world wouldn't get written.

—*Louis Phillips*

Michelle Pfeiffer skims magazines while waiting in line at the grocery store to get caught up on all the latest Hollywood gossip. That's funny in a way, since she was once a cashier at Vons herself.

We spend years of our lives waiting in line, waiting by the phone, waiting for others, waiting in "waiting rooms." Why not make that time work for you? Here are some suggestions:

- **Have tiny tasks to handle** while waiting for the laser printer or the Internet.

- **Make appointments well in advance** to get the most convenient time slots.

- **Drink tea or coffee before going to the doctor's office.** You know they're going to hand you a plastic cup, right?

- **Choose a health care provider with minimal paperwork hassles.**

- **I doodle on my idea pad,** look at goals, and write memos while waiting. Some of my best ideas have come during this "downtime."

- **Carry a folder with quick tasks,** surveys, requests, forms, invoices, reply cards.

- **Take a book with you to the movies and the doctor's office**—anywhere you're likely to have to wait for more than a few minutes.

WHAT CAN YOU DO IN TEN MINUTES OR LESS?

Clean your fingernails, leave messages for your mom/friends/lover/spouse, check/update your "to do" list/grocery list/errand list, update your calendar, go to the bathroom, do ten jumping jacks, fill out forms, go through the mail, water plants, make appointments, place an order, skim a magazine, check your e-mail, catnap, feed the fish, pet the cat, praise your kid, start the laundry, empty the dishwasher, drink a glass of water, find your keys, sew on a button, kiss somebody . . . You get the idea.

DRIVEN TO DISTRACTION

Have you ever thought about how much time you spend in your car? How much it costs? Divide your salary by the hours worked *plus the time spent commuting,* and that's your hourly wage. Scary, isn't it? Save some of that money by using some of the following tips:

- **Carpool** and have someone read the paper aloud on the way to work.

- **Use delivery services** rather than delivering things yourself. It actually costs less.

- **Work four-day weeks,** ten hours a day, if you can. It saves time (one less day to commute) and money (in gas, car maintenance, and clothing for one less day in the office).

- **Adjust your work times to avoid traffic.** Stop-and-go driving is much harder on your car (and your psyche). Also, going in early or staying late lets you get a lot done when the phone's not ringing.

- **Use cruise control** to save you time in court fighting speeding tickets (or having to work a second job just to pay your auto insurance).

- **Ask to telecommute** one or more days a week (twenty million do it). Telecommuting reduces costs in time, clothes, gas, wear and tear on your car and your body.

- **Use a microrecorder to make notes while you drive.** You can even take notes from books on tapes this way. Put key points on microtape, transcribe into written notes, or listen again later.

EMERGENCY MEASURES

The best way to deal with emergencies in your car is to avoid them. Fill up with gas *before* the gas gauge reaches empty. If you're running on fumes and late for work, you're probably also in the fast lane and nobody will let you get over until you're past the exit where the cheap gas is, and then you're really stressed and the car starts coughing and spitting and slowing down and the jerk behind you smacks right into you. (Not that it's ever happened to me.) But many ugly situations could be avoided by always having plenty of gas to get where you need to go the next day.

Remember, *plenty* of gas, taking into account that your gas gauge may be faulty. You never know when you may get lost, be forced to take a detour, or hit horrendous traffic. Don't let that be you walking along the side of the freeway in the rain, dejected, gas can in hand. Monster time-waster.

You have just joined the Boy/Girl Scouts, and you will be prepared. It's not hard, if you think ahead a little:

- **A spare key holder** (or a wire hanger, I guess) can be virtual lifesavers for the time when you lock the keys in your car—with the engine running!

- **Join an auto club** or roadside service group.

- **Check to see that you have a spare tire, jack, flares, tools, flashlight, and umbrella,** just in case. Yes, this sounds anal, but you only have to do it once a year (to make sure the flashlight batteries haven't gone dead and the tools haven't been stolen).

- **A cellular phone** lets you call ahead to notify people when you're running late, stuck in traffic, or out of gas. This may not save time, but it will definitely save some relationships and may save your job. A cellular phone also allows you to call the tow truck when the car breaks down so you don't have to find a call box or trudge to the nearest gas station—a major time-saver and quite possibly a lifesaver.

- **Be climatologically savvy.** A woman from Minneapolis told me she keeps a big bag of kitty litter in her car during the winter months. I'm from the Sunbelt, so I had to ask why. "Does this melt the snow?"

  "No," she answered politely. "The kitty litter provides traction when you're stuck in ice or snow." Who knew?

AUTO CONVENIENCES

Little conveniences in your car can make a big difference in saving time.

- **A cup holder prevents spills** (no extra time spent at the dry cleaners) and lets you take advantage of drive-through morning coffee.

- **A change holder (with coins in it) can get you past the** tollbooth quickly (no endless digging in pocket or purse for fifty cents while the drivers behind you honk). It can also save you the trouble of having to write a check for fifty cents when the change simply can't be found (while the drivers behind you go berserk). Don't top off your tank to get to an even dollar amount when you get gas, and stick the change in the coin holder. That way it's full when you need it.

- **Carry your current registration** and proof of insurance in the car—and make them easy to find in case you're pulled over. Having to go to court to show proof of registration is a colossal waste of time.

- **Having an auto notepad within reach** to write down my inspiration is a godsend. If you're left-handed, though, this won't work—there's no place to put it on the left side of the steering wheel.

- **Park it** *now.* Henry Herz, a game designer and Internet guru, advises, "Don't waste time looking for that perfect parking spot. Take the first one you see." How much time do you waste driving around in search of a spot only three spaces better than the first one you saw? On the other hand, time management expert Brian Tracy says, "If you believe there will be a parking spot right up front, *truly believe it,* one will appear." After hearing that, I drove to a crowded mall and thought positive thoughts. Like magic, a space appeared, right up front. Unbelievable, I thought! When I returned to my car I discovered a ticket on the windshield. I had parked in a loading zone. Oh, well. Next time, I'll stick to Henry's advice.

- **Don't be directionally impaired.** I, like many men, hate to ask for directions, so I keep a map in the car. Still, I'll frequently waste half an hour driving in circles, cursing at the map. Ask for help (or get a compass).

- **Stock your car with frequently needed items** like office supplies, toys and games, books on tape for the kids, and coupons for groceries and dining out. Handi Wipes are just that—handy. A trash bag is also a good idea.

IF IT AIN'T BROKE, KEEP IT THAT WAY

When you buy a car, read *Consumer Reports* to make sure your choice of vehicle has a good maintenance record. If you're buying a used car, have it thoroughly checked out by a mechanic first. Nothing is worse than being stuck in a repair shop, drinking bad coffee, and waiting for your car to be repaired—except maybe sitting by the side of the road waiting for the tow truck. A few other timely items to keep in mind (and keep you motoring along):

- **Have the oil changed** for you at one of those five-minute lube places. Do-it-yourselfers may disagree, but this saves a ton of time.

- **Keep up on the regular recommended services.** It's cheaper and will save you time in the long run. My best friend didn't have time to get his timing belt replaced. When the thing finally broke entirely, it caused other problems; he was left with a substantial repair bill and was without a car for over a week. I had to chauffeur him around. It's horrible seeing a grown man grovel for a ride.

- **Have your car repaired** while you're out of town. Especially if it's going to be a lengthy repair.

- **Keep a running list of problems** or symptoms you notice so that when you do take it in, you remember what needs to be done. This will save you a trip back later, once you remember the car makes a funny rattle when going over 100 mph.

- **Keep it clean.** Some people enjoy washing their car themselves. I can understand that. It's nice to see the fruits of your labor. I let the carwash do the bulk of the cleaning and then do the detail work myself. Same result, half the time.

- **If you keep track of mileage for tax reasons,** look for a mileage log that fits in your glove box and has a pocket for receipts as well.

- **Look for gas stations that allow you to swipe your credit card** rather than go inside to pay the attendant.

BEFORE AND AFTER

Carole, a single parent (recently divorced) with an eleven-year-old daughter and a nine-year-old son, is a radio talk show host with great hours (she's on air from nine A.M. to noon) but still never seems to have enough time to get everything done. She's exhausted and frazzled by the end of the day. She would like to work on a pilot for a TV show she's been developing, get in better shape, and improve the quality of her talk show.

We'll take a look at a typical weekday in her life and see where she can save time by following some of the tips included in this chapter.

MORNING

Problem: Alarm is set for seven A.M., but she always uses snooze button to extend to seven-thirty.

Solutions: Move alarm across the room, get to bed earlier, take a short nap before the kids come home from school.

Problem: Chaos reigns in the morning. She makes beds, fixes breakfast and kids' lunches, fights to get into bathroom to take a shower.

Solutions: Forget making beds or use a comforter, stagger bathroom times, teach kids how to make their own breakfast, fix lunches the night before.

Problem: She walks the dog while kids shower and gets depressed noticing dead plants, uncut lawn.

Solution: Hire a neighbor teen to walk dog and mow lawn.

Problem: She takes too long to put on makeup, blow-dry and tease hair, decide what to wear.

Solutions: Put hair up (it's radio, not TV). Lay clothes out the night before and simplify what she wears (solid colors, minimal accessories).

Problem: It's a scramble to drop kids at school on her way to work.

Solution: Leave five minutes earlier. She likes to spend this time with kids, but it needs to be unfrazzled time, giving them a chance to touch base before their day starts.

Problem: She arrives at the station five minutes before the show starts, with no time to prepare or meet guests. She's rushed, stressed, and flustered—no way to start a show. At news break she runs to lunchroom and grabs a doughnut and coffee.

Solutions: Get up earlier and eat breakfast and do her prep at home. She can't arrive much earlier because she drops the kids off at school, but she can delegate more to her producer—who, it turns out, wants more responsibility.

Problem: During the show, the producer is busy behind the scenes.

Solutions: She enlists the help of a (free) intern to take calls, sort mail, and type letters during the hours the show is on the air.

AFTERNOON

Problem: After the show, she retreats to her cubicle to send thank-yous to guests, birthday cards to past guests, return calls, and plan future shows.

Solutions: With the intern's help, she has a fraction of the mail and calls to take care of.

Problem: She spends an hour or two hanging around and joking with crew and producer, does promos. She calls the next day's guest or their publicist, gives directions, grabs a pizza for lunch.

Solutions: She and producer go for a forty-five-minute walk and eat lunch while discussing upcoming show ideas.

Then she does her promos. The intern or producer calls the upcoming guest and faxes them a preprinted map.

Problem: She rushes to pick up kids at school, takes her daughter to violin lessons (she forgot the violin, so they rush home to pick it up), takes her son to his Little League practice (he forgot his glove, so they rush back home to get it). Then she runs to the bank, grocery store, and dry cleaners while waiting to pick up her kids.

Solutions: Picks up kids and comes home. Hires a violin instructor to come to house, while son carpools with teammate. Brings press kits, other reading materials for her show while waiting to pick up her son and his teammate, banks by mail, uses a dry cleaner that picks up and delivers, stocks up on groceries by buying in bulk and using a full-size freezer.

Problem: More errands with kids, grocery store, video store, mall.

Solutions: Group all errands into one or two days a week. With the other new changes, she has time.

EVENING

Problem: Returns home to a machine full of messages she can't get to and hurriedly starts dinner before she has to get ready to give a speech that night. While she's dressing, the phone rings, and a telemarketer wastes five minutes (she hates to be rude). Baby-sitter arrives, and there's no time to help kids with homework.

Solutions: Order a pizza (just this once) or go over speech while cooking. Get a cellular phone to check messages and call back while in car. Cut off the telemarketer with a *polite* "No, thank you" and hang up or, better still, get an unlisted number.

Problem: Grabs only outfit that's not dirty and finds a button missing. Panic attack!

Solution: Lay outfit out beforehand and check for spots, missing buttons, matching accessories.

Problem: Baby-sitter is new, and she has to explain rules, write down important numbers.

Solution: Write out instructions once and make copies.

Problem: Arrives at talk late and unprepared. The person introducing her calls her "Joan" and gets the call letters of her station wrong.

Solutions: Hire a speaker's bureau to handle engagements, set up luncheon speeches where possible, have copy of a standard introduction to give the emcee.

Problem: Arrives home and discovers she has no money to pay sitter.

Solution: Keep a petty cash stash.

Problem: It's now late and she still has to clean up spare room and bathrooms for houseguests arriving tomorrow.

Solutions: Turn spare room into an office so there's no room for guests and/or hire a maid (she hates to clean).

Problem: Falls into bed well after the *Tonight* show has ended.

Solutions: Take a long bath, read, and turn in by ten.

Time Saved: One to two hours *every day.*

With her new time management style and newfound time, Carole is

1. dating again (this was her top priority, not mine).

2. spending more quality time with her kids.

3. taking a nap in the afternoon, catching up on sleep.

4. seeing an occasional movie and reading more for pleasure.

5. working on developing her TV show idea.

10

• • • • •

LOST AND FOUND

Improving Your Memory

First you forget names, then you forget faces, then you forget to zip up your fly, and then you forget to unzip your fly.

—*Branch Rickey*

Has this ever happened to you? You're doing something you really enjoy, and you feel great. Everything is right with the world at that moment. Then, gradually, an ugly, sinking feeling starts to creep into your consciousness. Your hands start to get clammy, your head begins to pound. Something is wrong, very wrong, but what is it?

Then it hits you like a ton of bricks.

We can end this story with any one of the following scenarios (and then some):

1. You suddenly realize you were supposed to meet a client at your office over an hour ago.

2. You suddenly realize you were supposed to pick up someone at the airport earlier that day. Worse still, you don't even remember who it is!

3. You've been on vacation for over a week when you suddenly realize you forgot to call someone to come over and feed your bird. (Ouch!)

Does this make you a bad person? Of course not. It happens to the best of us, some more often than others. In many cases, however, these ugly incidents could have been avoided. Which is good news, considering the damage a selective memory can do to our careers, friendships, and even our pets.

Blanking on someone's name, missing an appointment, forgetting to follow through on crucial details, or falsely accusing others can leave people thinking you are unreliable, unintelligent, unfriendly, uncaring, or even dishonest—which can leave them understandably angry and upset. Becoming chronically forgetful is certainly not going to win you a promotion or many new friends.

It's also very stressful on you, not to mention extremely embarrassing. Worse still, it can be very dangerous. Losing your keys, forgetting to lock the door behind you, or failing to turn off the iron can all have dire consequences. There's the true story of a veteran free-fall photographer who remembered to strap on all his camera equipment and jumped out of a plane without his parachute. (Think about that one for a minute.)

Yet there are some creative people who actually *want* to be seen as absentminded. They mistakenly think it's charming or eccentric. "Hey, I'm an artist, so it's expected of me." Maybe you can get away with that excuse with your parents, but others see it differently.

When is forgetfulness a sign of something more serious?

If you forget where you parked your car after an exciting event, that's not a problem. When you forget if you drove yourself there or not, *that's* a problem.

What is considered normal?

A classified ad in a major metropolitan newspaper read "I would like to thank all the millions of people who helped look for my stolen van. I remember where I left it."

WHY WE LOSE MEMORY

I can't memorize the words by themselves. I have to memorize the feelings.

—*Marilyn Monroe*

Now . . . where was I? Right, the causes for memory loss, and there are many. As you look at this partial list, keep in mind that by nature, creative people are more susceptible to some of these causes than the average person.

- Trying to balance too many things at once.
- Information overload.
- Too much stress.
- Lack of focus.
- Lack of sleep.
- Alcohol or substance abuse.
- A hectic, chaotic lifestyle.
- Not writing things down.
- Disorganization.

Creative people have a unique kind of memory. They can remember the look or feel of something they came in contact with as a child but are often unable to recall where they put their keys five minutes ago. It's a strange phenomenon that can make everyday living frustrating but in other ways is beneficial to their art.

The richness and vividness of past experiences tend to surface while in the throes of work. Artist Alice Neel said, "In 1973, I sent my brain back to 1915 and I managed to remember flowers—and paint them—as I had seen them then. Quite a feat. And the flowers were fresher."

HOW TO IMPROVE YOUR MEMORY

The journey of a thousand miles must begin with wondering if you turned off the iron.

—William Rotsler

Use it or lose it. Recent research shows that mice brains actually add neurons when the mice are kept in a rich, active, learning environment. The implication is clear. The act of thinking, and particularly the multilevel kind of thinking that we call "creative," can actually increase the capacity of your brain.

Even at birth, our brains are amazing, with a complex organization that allows us to function in many ways better than any computer. You can use this neurological organization—without having to get an M.D.—to help you remember things you really need to remember. It's called the "whole-brain approach." Put simply, the more places you can stick a memory in your brain, the more likely it is that you'll be able to find it later.

Use all your senses. Say it out loud, write it down, trace the words with your finger, listen carefully, attach related meanings to it—particularly visual or aural (sound) ones. Make as many connections as possible.

REMEMBERING NAMES AND NUMBERS

I know very few creative people who are good at remembering names or numbers, although many are extremely good at remembering faces or physical details. Use this trait by making a visual connection to the name: Bob is short; Carole has carrot red hair; Sam is the guy in the green shirt. It doesn't have to make sense to anyone but you (Sam/green eggs and ham). This is just to provide a cross-filing reference for your brain.

Try to slow down the meeting process, especially if you're meeting a lot of people at once. Ask for a business card, look at it, note anything different about the card that you can connect to the name/person. There's nothing wrong with asking someone you just met to repeat their name, listening intently—and it helps even more if you repeat it after them. You'll notice that expert schmoozers always do this.

When you have a little more time or you're meeting only one new person, you can extend the process. Make the name into a rhyme or jingle (but not out loud); attaching music—even three or four notes—to a name can make it much easier to remember. Play around with the name, say it to yourself a couple of times, use it in a sentence, make an acronym of it. When you say good-bye, use their name and focus on their features. Write it down as soon as possible afterward.

- **Always write down both the name and number** when you're talking to someone new on the phone. Put both in your Rolodex or address file as soon as possible, repeating it out loud along with who they are and why you spoke with them.

- **It helps to make associations when you're trying to remember numbers.** I did this once when I didn't have any paper to write down a phone number. The first three numbers worked out to be the same as my brother's birthday; the next two were the same as the year I graduated from high school; and the last two numbers were the year my car was built: 431-8390. Easy!

- **Shorten long names or numbers:** NBC, ALA, 2-double 3-ninety-six.

- **Break it down.** They say seven is the limit to the number of things we can remember at one time. It's no coincidence that phone numbers are seven digits long. The more you can chunk a number down, the easier it will be to remember. A phone number is really only four numbers: 619-555-53-12. Social Security is really three numbers: 150-12-8283.

REMEMBERING THINGS TO DO

Don't expect to remember everything—nobody needs the kind of mind clutter that would involve. You can give yourself reminders in many ways or eliminate the need to remember by developing habits (so you don't have to think about it) or setting things up so that memory isn't an issue.

- **Make a date.** Writer Franny Van Nevel has a great tip: Tie things like your annual physical to important dates like your birthday. I heard a grocery clerk say, "I started working here the day before my birthday six years ago—I'll always remember it because I had to work on my birthday!"

- **An alarm on your watch** or computer is better than a string on your finger. Set it for an hour before you have to be somewhere, to give you plenty of time to get ready and go. Or set it for the same time each day to remind you to get up out of your chair and stretch.

- **There are cool little devices that help you remember important things.** Use a pill box with compartments for each day of the week so you remember whether you took your pills or not—as long as you remember what day this is.

- **Use Post-it notes** and stick them on your purse, wrap them around your keys, paste them to the bathroom mirror, phone, refrigerator, or computer. Get it in your face. You can use this to remind others, too. Just remember, this "in your face" stuff can get irritating if it comes from anyone other than yourself.

- **Put things in your path** so you trip over them and can't forget. This doesn't work for breakable things, and it won't always leave you in a great mood when you've fallen flat, but if it works . . .

- **Visualize your day before you leave the house.** See yourself at the meeting, what is in front of you, what you're doing. Aha, I need my notes for my presentation, a pen and paper to write, and my microrecorder!

- **Put your watch on the opposite wrist** or a ring on the opposite finger as a reminder that you need to remember something. I personally don't care for this one much—I go nuts trying to remember what I'm supposed to remember.

- **Organize.** I know a young art student who was forgetting something that he needed for class every day. Although he got in great shape, running back to the dorm and then racing to class, his tardiness was becoming a problem. He figured the best way to combat his forgetfulness was to set up routines, doing things the same way every time. It may sound rigid, but this was self-defense. Now he always puts everything for one class in one pile, for the next class in another pile; as soon as he's finished working on a project, he puts everything from the project in the appropriate class pile. When he leaves in the morning, he simply picks up his piles for the classes he has that day. He says the simple repetition helps him to avoid leaving stuff out.

- **The act of making a list or Mind Mapping can trigger your memory.** By writing things down, you're engaging another part of your brain, making another connection, and opening yourself to more connections. List making can be very creative, becoming almost a word association tool.

REMEMBERING WHERE YOU PUT THINGS

"Hey, where are my glasses?"
"They're on your nose."
"Be more specific!"

—*Jimmy Durante*

My friend Steve is always having to find things for his wife. She puts them away "in the logical place"—but her logic tends to change from day to day. Try the following tips (or call Steve):

- **It helps to keep some things in more than one place.** Have backups. Carry a small vial of pills with you. Keep a spare set of keys hidden outside your house and another set on a hook near the door inside the house.

- **Group like things together.** Things you use together, store together. Put all the housecleaning and car-washing stuff in one cupboard with sponges, rags, bucket, broom, and mop, all the laundry stuff—coat hangers, detergent, bleach, fabric softener and laundry bag—above or next to the washing machine.

- **Stop for a second and look where you are leaving something before you set it down.** Concentrate. Say it aloud. Take a mental picture, a snapshot. When you park your car, don't just look at the cars around it— look at the light posts, see where you are in relation to buildings or exits, check the name or level of the parking garage. Repeat it to yourself or say it to whomever you're with. "Okay, we're in A-nine, straight back from the main entrance."

- **Mark your calendar when you lend something out.** Note what it is, whom you lent it to, and when you should get it back. A friend of mine came up to me a couple of months ago and handed me a check for $200. "What's this for?" I blurted out, surprised. "You lent it to me last summer. Sorry it took so long to pay you back," he replied. He could have never paid me back and I wouldn't have been any the wiser—I'd forgotten all about it. Thank goodness for honest friends!

- **When working on my car, I take a Polaroid snapshot before taking anything apart.** If you're working on shelves or furniture, put the screws in a plastic bag with the instructions, and label the bag. Others like to lay things out in the order they were removed or even number them with those all-purpose Post-it notes.

REMEMBERING EVERYTHING ELSE

Studies of memory show that different people have different memory "triggers." Some people remember best aurally (if they hear it), some tactilely (if they touch it or write it), some verbally (if they say it), and some visually (if they see or read it). If you think about it, you can probably figure out which type of input you retain best.

I do well with hearing—so I like lectures and talks and I frequently listen to tapes of books, lectures, or my own verbal notes while I'm driving. I have a friend who's hopeless at remembering things she hears—a real "in one ear and out the other" kind of person. At meetings and lectures she takes written notes—which help her remember what's been said even if she never refers to her notes again. And she listens to music in her car.

Recognizing your memory "style" can help you, but don't let it limit you. If you remember things best when you hear them, make sure you hear what you need to remember—tape it and play it over. But don't neglect the other senses—the more memory triggers you can involve, the more likely you are to hit the target when you need to.

- **Use a tickler or a master list of things you want to remember.** Just the act of writing them down will help. Writing in longhand is better than typing into a computer—it's much more tactile. Either way, periodically reading over your tickler file or master list (reading it out loud and following the letters with your finger) will help you remember things even better.

- **Visualize.** I travel a lot, giving lectures, and I've found some pretty neat little restaurants. Unfortunately it's hard to remember where they are when I don't get back to a particular town for a year or so. So I visualize the street, driving down it in my mind. I see the front of the restaurant—and I know where it is!

- **Remember patterns and shapes.** The parking garage at Horton Plaza, a unique shopping mall in downtown San Diego, uses fruits and vegetables to name each level. Somehow it's easier to remember I'm on pineapple or avocado (that's so California, isn't it?) than that I'm parked on level three or seven.

- **Keep a standing checklist for regular appointments.** Also put down things you do often, and then add to the list as you notice things you need to remember. I keep a travel checklist that includes stop mail, cancel paper, set timers, buy film, check tickets, and so on.

- **Write things on your calendar.** Simply including the due date for my library books saved me a bundle last year. (Those daily fines add up!)

- **List important dates on your calendar.** Transfer the dates from year to year. Birthdays, anniversaries, the Joneses' annual Fourth of July pool party—all can go into your calendar right at the start of the year.

- **Repetition helps.** That's why teachers have you write "I will not swear in class" fifty times on the chalkboard. By the end, the words are embedded in your brain.

- **Write it with your other hand.** This involves a whole other area of your brain. It doesn't matter if you can't read it. The simple act of writing is what's important.

- **Make associations.** If you do any sailing, you know a boat has a port and a starboard side. It's not always easy to remember which is the right side and which is the left. The port side is the left side. How do I remember? Both port and left have four letters; starboard has more.

- **Tell someone else.** You really learn a subject when you teach it to someone.

- **Studies show that you retain things learned just before you go to sleep.** The theory is that because your body is relaxed, your mind is more receptive. You can use this concept in two ways: study before bed, or do relaxation exercises before you study.

- **When you're trying to remember something complex, organize and break it down.** It doesn't matter *how* you organize or break it down—just find a way to cut it into bite-size pieces.

- **Some people have longer attention spans than others,** but we all have a limit. That's why half-hour TV shows work so well and three-hour movies consistently fail, why plays have acts, why good lecturers give breaks.

Your memory reaches a point of diminishing returns. Try to be aware of where that point is for you, then work in shorter sessions.

- **Put things you need to remember into a story.** We remember stories. Facts tell, but stories sell.

LONG-TERM MEMORY

My parents, Annette and Harvey, are both in their early sixties. My mom is always complaining about my father's selective memory. When my mom noticed they were offering free memory testing as part of an ongoing research program, she signed my dad up. A couple of weeks into the program, I asked my dad how it was going. I knew someone who might also be interested in participating.

So I said, "Hey, Dad, what's the doctor's name who is running that memory program you're in?"

He gave me one of those blank stares. "The doctor's name? Hmmm . . . I need help with this one. What's that thing called that you hit the ball over in volleyball?"

"A net?" I replied.

"Yes, that's it!" he exclaimed. "Hey, Annette! What's the name of that doctor I go to?"

Long-term memory operates on many of the same principles as short-term memory, but it is stored differently in the brain. Many people, as they reach old age, lose some of their short-term memory capability, while things that happened forty years ago come back clear as a bell. In middle age, however, long-term memory often takes a backseat and becomes harder and harder to access. You can offset this in many of the same ways we've already talked about. The more associations you can make, the more likely you are to remember something. If you give it meaning, give it importance, take it in deeply, associate it with something important, you'll remember it for a long time. Bill Gates still remembers hundreds of lines of source code for his original BASIC programming language.

● ●

When you are asked to stand and introduce yourself in a group setting, don't begin with your name. The first few things you say generally go unheard because people are busy sizing you up. Say something like "I am a writer who helps children reach their full potential by building up their self-esteem. My books include *Positively Mother Goose* and *Full Esteem Ahead*. My name is Diane Loomans."

● ●

LOST AND FOUND

About nine out of ten U.S. homes have TV remote controls; eight of ten report losing it. The remote is usually found

1. in/under furniture.
2. in the kitchen or bathroom.
3. in bed.
4. in the refrigerator.

Study by Magnavox

We have all misplaced things at one time or another. But if you are chronically losing or misplacing things, this could be a symptom that you are overwhelmed and under a great deal of stress. It may be that you are rushing too fast and not paying attention; in that case, you need to slow down.

According to the Harper Index, a year of your life is wasted looking for misplaced things. A year! (One of the big excuses for being late is "I couldn't find my keys.")

When you misplace something, eventually it turns up. Losing something for good is much more serious and can have dire consequences to the creative person. Consider this story as a worst-case scenario: In the 1920s Hemingway was to meet up with his wife, Hadley, in Europe. While en route, she left a suitcase containing virtually all his stories and poems (both originals and carbon copies) unattended, and it was stolen. This left Hemingway no option but to rewrite everything that was lost.

Here are several suggestions that can save you the frustration and heartache of losing or misplacing things in the future:

- **Hooks** are ideal for things that would otherwise be lost in the clutter on the floor.

- **Affix or keep together pairs of things** that always seem to get separated. Stuff your gloves in your coat pocket.

- **For kids, pin socks together,** tape their signed permission slip to their schoolbooks the night before, put completed homework in their books or backpack.

- **Let there be light!** Could it be there isn't adequate lighting to see things in your closets, trunk, or work space?

- **Having a designated, consistent place where you keep like things** is the best tip of all. Tape a label to the shelf, closet, cupboard, hook, or whatever to help you remember what goes there. If the labels embarrass you, tape them on the underside of the shelf, the inside of the cupboard or closet door.

- **Take a couple of minutes at the end of the day or after completing a project to clean up.** It saves all kinds of time, considering how long it can take to hunt for lost things.

- **Attach an index card with a list of what's in every box you store.** Any kind of label on a box that you can't see in, or that is stuffed to the brim with junk, saves time. Having to pull down the box and empty it, only to discover that the item you are looking for isn't there, is a waste of time.

- **Group related things together in boxes,** like "Holiday Stuff" or "Winter Clothes." Don't forget those labels.

- **I tape instruction manuals to the bottom of items.** If it stops working or I need to adjust it, I just turn it over and know that the manual is there. The premise behind this is twofold: keep things where you use them, and make it easy to find it when you need it.

KEYS

- **Have a special place** you keep them, either a hook, bowl, or attached to a tab in your purse. Make sure they always return to the same place when not in use.

- **Have two extra sets** of keys made. Give a set to a friend or relative, stash another set in a safe place that you can access in an emergency.

- **Get a beeper attachment** for your keys that you can activate when they are misplaced.

- **Never spend more than a minute searching** for your keys. Grab your spare set and look for them later.

- **Label the keys** to lockers, suitcases, and other miscellaneous locks with a hanging tag, and make a key rack to keep them from being lost or misplaced.

- **Color code your keys** with key caps or use a key light to reduce fumbling. I put a key cap on the house key so I can feel the raised bumps in the dark.

- **I have a distinctive key chain** that makes my keys hard to lose and includes my first name and phone number, which has saved me on several occasions. Don't put your address on your keys, however—it's an invitation to thieves.

GLASSES

- **Keep them near** where they are used.
- **Use a chain** so they "hang around" when not in use.
- **Have spare pairs** made.

PAPERS

- **Keep tickets** to an event in your tickler file or pinned to a bulletin board.
- **Keep gift certificates** with you or in your car.
- **Coupons** go into a coupon file or envelope.

PENS

- **Have one tethered near the phone.**
- **Buy in bulk** and put several in places where they are frequently needed.

PHONE NUMBERS

- **Keep these in a safe, dry, central place.**
- **Enter new or updated phone numbers** into your address book right away, or keep a file for phone numbers waiting to be entered into your computer.

MEMENTOS

- **Have a single clean, dry, safe place** to keep old letters, photos, and mementos. I have a friend who uses the drawers in her linen closet for this kind of thing. She only has one spare set of sheets and towels, but that's all she needs.

TOOLS AND SPORTS EQUIPMENT

- **Don't lend them out.** If you do, drop a sticky note or index card in your toolbox to remind yourself what you loaned to whom.
- **Brand your stuff.** All my buddy's tools have a small spot of fluorescent paint on them. Even when we're working side by side, he can quickly identify his tools.
- **Keep like sports equipment together** rather than scattered in several places. As with tools, if you lend something out, drop an index card in your equipment box indicating what you loaned and who you loaned it to.

Scavenger Hunt

In ten minutes or less, could you locate, if you had to, any of the following items?

Dictionary, keys, Band-Aid, pen, business card, glasses, an AA battery, birth certificate, instruction manual for the VCR, vacuum bag, medical records, umbrella, film, safety pin, sales receipt for your computer, spare light bulb, recipes, hairpiece, car registration, *TV Guide*, past three years' tax returns?

11
. . . . .
THE BIG "O"

Organizing Ideas

I'm a pack rat and I devoutly believe in pack ratting. I can't tell you how many times some little nugget of information—buried deep in my overloaded brain and in some folder someplace—will occur to me and provide the missing link that ties together everything I'm working on. I figure the efficiency of this process is about two percent, but that's all right. I don't mind the messiness.

—Tom Peters

Life is messy, and there isn't always time to clean up. The creative person's life should be rich, filled with fun and interesting things to do—the least of which is organizing and cleaning up. Neat does *not* equal organized. You can be neat and orderly and still disorganized. On the other hand, too much of anything, especially clutter, isn't healthy.

Clutter, stuff, and piles (the kind you keep on your desk, the table, the floor, the chair) aren't necessarily bad. You can squirrel away your little tchotchkes (a Yiddish term for trinkets), keep that oddball stuff on your desk, and continue to toss your clothes over a chair. But be honest, now. Has your disorganization been the source of an argument with a spouse, co-worker, or roommate recently? Have you "misplaced" something in the past week, only to find it buried under a pile of other misplaced things? Are you finding that the clutter in your life has become a burden?

For many people, a certain amount of clutter is stimulating. For most, however, too much clutter is a distraction. How much is too much? It's an individual thing, but recognize that you're likely to be more sensitive to your surroundings than most, and messiness, clutter, and dirt can have a negative impact on your psyche without your even realizing it.

Leaving something out and within reach is great—if you use that item on a regular basis. If you use it only twice a year, put it away, for cryin' out loud! If an item makes your life better, easier, is nice to look at, and/or has value to you, keep it wherever it's most useful.

You may find that old sketches or pictures or photos spark ideas for current projects. Don't leave them in piles—fill your walls with them. You may find that old toys or family mementos bring fond childhood memories flooding back—or they may elicit painful but helpful reminders. Make a memory case or special shelf and keep them out where you see them every day—keep those memories alive! Don't leave them buried where they can ambush you and take your time and thoughts away when you're hunting for something else.

I have an old, rusted dive knife that I still store with my scuba gear. Whenever I go diving, it reminds me of the time I was tangled in kelp near the end of a dive and nearly out of air. I kept my head and didn't panic, cut myself free, and survived. Although I don't use that knife anymore, it is a constant reminder to stay calm and stay close to your dive buddy.

Lighten up! We're not born neat (or disorganized). You are not a failure if everything in your life isn't in order, nor inferior to those whose lives are organized down to every last detail. Many extremely talented and intelligent people have struggled with this. Be realistic. The goal isn't and shouldn't be to have a perfectly immaculate office or home. Set standards you can achieve and maintain. As writer Karen Mynatt put it, "Clean enough to live in, dirty enough to be happy." Devise a system that will work for you.

- You buy things you already have.
- You trip and hurt yourself.
- You are constantly looking for the TV remote.
- You miss deadlines.
- You borrow things and never return them.
- You show up unprepared.
- You are seen as forgetful, unreliable, unsanitary.
- You have no room to work.
- You need to rent extra storage space.
- Your clutter is a burden to you.
- Your mess becomes dangerous (toxic).

SUCCESS STORIES

When less expensive "knockoff" versions of clothing designer Nicole Miller's designs threatened to ruin her upcoming collection, she decided to revamp her designs. She replaced her trademark splashy prints with fabric in solid colors. Not wanting to discard the unused splashy fabric, she used the material to make men's ties, which became an enormous hit and later her trademark. Miller, a frequent traveler, says she saves everything from wherever she goes—beer bottles, matchbooks, theater programs—and uses them to inspire her designs. Her ties have featured tabloid headlines, Elvis, and Oreo cookies.

Actor David Duchovny, Agent Mulder on the hit TV show *The X-Files*, has been the subject of many tabloid rumors, many of which are inaccurate. "There was a story about me being a neat freak. I'm actually pretty sloppy," he told *Cosmopolitan* magazine. "I couldn't deny I'd never had sex, but I could deny that I'd never been neat."

Beethoven was a slob. His rooms were a mess, his handwriting was sloppy, and he himself was so untidy that he was once arrested as a tramp by accident. But it didn't affect his art form, did it? Or did it? He spent enormous amounts of time hiring and firing housekeepers (he didn't trust them) and rewriting scores that were lost or stained or torn. He was seen as an eccentric by his patrons and potential patrons—many of whom refused to give him commissions because he was so socially "difficult." His health was affected, and he died relatively young, cutting short a brilliant career.

• •

Jot down the first three words that come into your head to describe your work environment. (If you included words like "cyclone," "disaster," or "condemned" in your description, don't worry. There is hope.)

• •

THE PROBLEMS CLUTTER CAUSES

We can keep busy rearranging the deck chairs on the sinking Titanic, but this ignores the obvious problem.
—Dr. Eric Allenbaugh

Keeping things in piles works only if you regularly go through your minimountains of stuff. That's the only way to know what's there and to make use of it. Do you really have the desire/time/energy to do that?

Clutter costs. You have to store it (rent extra space), maintain it (wash and repair), move it around (make room for more), and go through it. There can be other, less obvious costs as well: strain on business and personal relationships, loss of mental clarity, loss of or damage to valuable items, increase in daily stress and frustration.

EXCESSIVE CLUTTER CAN CAUSE PAIN AND STRAIN IN YOUR LIFE

- **You no longer feel comfortable in your home or office;** your environment is no longer cozy or nurturing—it's just plain dirty.

- **You've no room to work anymore**—your stuff takes up all your space (at a whopping $100 per square foot).

- **You end up with a strained back** (moving stuff around) and strained relationships (there is all that nagging to deal with)—plus piles of junk are a major turnoff in the bedroom.

- **Clutter often causes embarrassment** (clients, boss, mother-in-law, your dates)—if not to you, then to your significant other.

- **It litters your life and clogs your mind.** No matter what you say, there's a point past which clutter is *not* creative or conducive to creativity.

- **It can leave you overwhelmed** and feeling constantly under pressure, literally weighted down.

- **Clutter can hurt your image**—you're likely to be seen by others as disorganized, unreliable, someone who can't get it together or let go of life's detritus.

- **You can't enjoy free time or relax** when you look around and see things that make you feel guilty because you never finished or followed through on them. This is a constant source of negativity that can be very discouraging, eroding your natural creativity, clarity, and peace of mind.

- **Serious clutter could be a sign of deeper problems**—living in the past, an inability to let go physically or emotionally, a childish defiance of authority (Mom wants you to clean your room), depression.

- **Clutter is often more distracting than inspiring,** interfering with creativity, diverting thoughts and energy. Author Stephanie Winston calls this "visual noise."

CLUTTER CAN WASTE YOUR TIME

- **You can't find what you need** when you need it.
- **It takes much more time to clean** a cluttered office or home.
- **If you share space with anyone,** you've spent time arguing about your stuff, your clutter, your messiness.
- **You waste a lot of time making decisions on clutter**—keep it or not, go through it or not, move it or not, put it where?
- **You probably don't realize how much time it takes to protect it,** worry about it, maintain it, move it, or store it.

• •

Factoid

The main complaint about living with another person: Sloppiness.

• •

Factoid

According to a recent survey, the rooms that cleaning services find the messiest are

1. family room.
2. kid's room.
3. kitchen.
4. master bedroom.
5. bathroom.

SURVEY CONDUCTED FOR MAID BRIGADE

• •

LEARNING TO LET GO

*Have nothing in your house that you do not know to
be useful or believe to be beautiful.*

—Henry David Thoreau

I know several people who are clean but not neat. Their homes are spotless, as long as you don't look in the closet or under the bed. These people are no more organized, or disorganized, than those who like to leave things lying around. There must be a healthy balance between the two.

We were playing poker at a friend's home when the power went out. All you could see was the orange glow of several cigars. Soon his wife entered the smoke-filled room and asked, "Where's the flashlight?"

"It's in the junk drawer, dear," came the reply.

Frustrated, she called back, "Could you be a little more specific?"

A good organizing system is easy to look at, easy to maintain, practical, and functional (which means you can find what you need when you need it), while still letting the personality of the person come through. Although getting organized and cleaning out the clutter in our lives can be difficult at first, eventually it will turn into a painless, pleasant, and positive experience for you (and those around you).

Think of shedding clutter like shedding clothing. To get more comfortable after work, don't you strip off the layers of formal wear and slip on your favorite sweatpants, T-shirt, and slippers? It doesn't matter how you look to others, it feels great, free. In the same way, your space (both at work and at home) should feel free and comfortable, without too much concern for what others think.

If you want to feel even freer, you can strip down to the bare essentials. For some this is liberating; others feel, well, naked. For this reason, it's a good idea to take it slowly (striptease?). Imagine you're on one end of a teeter-totter and all your stuff is on the other end. Don't throw out everything at once. You're likely to need the comfort of at least a few things lying around. Go for balance.

Think of it this way:

- Clearing out means you'll have more room for newer and better stuff!
- Selling it off can help you pay for a vacation you've wanted to take.
- Giving it away feeds the soul.
- Space makes life more livable.

WHY WE BECOME PACK RATS

One person's junk is another person's treasure. That's crap. One person's junk is another person's junk, period!

—Lee Silber

I can remember when I was young, watching the popular television comedy, *Sanford and Son,* starring Redd Foxx as the proud owner of a salvage company. I never thought the show was all that funny, probably because its premise of a father and son who argue over clutter hit too close to home.

I would be the "son" in *Sanford and Son.* I am the child of pack rats. When I was growing up, all the drawers in our home were junk drawers. To give you an idea how bad things were (are), my parents maintain a storage unit to hold all their overflow stuff, much of it decades old. I refer to this junk as "B.C." (Before we moved to California in 1975).

Here are a few of the items they pay to keep in their storage unit:

- Tennis balls (and they don't even play tennis).
- Cool Whip containers filled with rusty used nails that my dad spent days hammering to straighten.
- Boxes and boxes of dried-up pens.

- A broken black and white TV (black and white!).
- A cash register (empty cash drawer; I checked).
- Just the other day, my dad proudly showed me an old drill (clearly B.C.) that was heavily wrapped in electrical tape. He'd spent the entire weekend fixing it. Before he demonstrated it to me, he warned, "Don't worry about that burning smell, but be careful, there's no on or off switch." *Dad!*

My concern, as a child of pack rats, is whether I have a predisposition for becoming a pack rat, or is this a recessive gene that skips a generation? If it's recessive, does that mean my children could be pack rats?

Are You a Pack Rat?

To begin with, the words *"pack rat"* themselves don't have the nicest connotation, do they? Picture a big, ugly rodent, digging through junk and then dragging stuff back to its nest, leaving little droppings along the way.

Is it all that bad? I guess it depends on whom you ask.

Answer a simple "That could be me" or "No way!" to the following scenarios:

- The local library frequently calls you to look up articles from your magazine collection dating back to 1948.
- When the blue light at Kmart starts flashing, you feel all funny inside and rush to buy whatever's on special, whether you need it or not.
- You have coffee cans filled with more fasteners than Home Depot.
- You've had an argument with someone about who had more junk, and you won.
- You had to rent a storage unit to hold all your junk . . . er, "valued possessions."

- A well-meaning friend inadvertently threw away a piece of your clutter and you are still not speaking to him, two years later.

- When shopping for a home, your first priority is how much storage space it has.

- Others in the neighborhood come to you whenever they need a spare part.

- People call you before they hang their signs to announce an upcoming garage sale to offer you first dibs, hoping you'll clean them out.

(More than one "That could be me" answer is cause for serious concern.)

Now have a friend or significant other take the same quiz on your behalf. Compare answers, and be humble.

THE PACK RAT MENTALITY

There is a pack rat psychology, although it's not very flattering. It's connected to a Depression-era mentality, which explains my parents' inability to throw away anything with any possible potential use. During the Depression, when you didn't know where your next nickel was coming from, it made sense to store things you might need someday. Buying new was not an option.

You don't have to have lived through the Depression to have this need to hoard against an uncertain future. I have a friend whose grandmother lived for garage sales. She bought anything that was a "deal," whether it was broken or not, whether she needed it or not. She bought clothing in all sizes, men's and women's and children's, tattered or nearly new. For the last decade of her life she was forced to have a continuous garage sale of her own, because her stuff had overflowed her house, her garage, and her yard, and the only way to make room for the junk she was still buying was to sell some of the junk she had. As a child, my friend found this enormously embarrassing, but she now understands. Her grandmother came to a new country with nothing but the clothes on her back, and the fear of destitution that drove her to work hard and build a nest egg then kept driving her for the rest of her life. She needed constantly to protect herself against having nothing, even though she died a wealthy woman.

I've even seen pack rat mentality surface in a cat (pack cat?). My neighbor found a scraggly half-grown kitten hanging around their yard a couple of years ago. They took her in and fed her, and she grew into a wonderful companion. She's also the only truly fat cat I know. Unlike most of her kind, she'll eat whether she needs to or not, and she lets you know if dinnertime passes and fresh food isn't set down for her. I really believe she never got over her near starvation as a kitten and instinctively guards against ever going hungry again.

Pack rats tend to become emotionally attached to possessions (even those they borrowed from others, which is why they're not good at returning things). Insecurities can be the reason behind wanting to keep all those old trophies, ribbons, and grade school report cards, but there's nothing wrong with that. If you need reminders of the good things you did, keep them! Set them out where you can see them, where they provide motivation. If they're in a box somewhere at the bottom of the closet, they're not going to alleviate your insecurity or provide inspiration. If you don't want to display them, you don't need them.

Admittedly, some mementos are physically hard to display. It might be too big and awkward to fit anywhere, even if you had room for it. In that case, take a picture of it and display the picture.

Other things are equally hard to store, and it's easier just to leave them out because you have to move the car, get out a ladder, and shift several boxes before you can put them away. These require hard decisions. Do you want it out? Use that creativity and find a way to make it pretty or useful. If you put it away in the garage attic behind other boxes, will you remember it's there when (and if) you need it? If not, don't store it.

Waffling on decisions is a key reason why things begin to pile up. You can't decide where it should go, so you leave it lying around or chuck it into a "holding" pile, which will likely become its permanent home. Before you know it, that "holding pile" has had offspring and you're facing a serious overpopulation problem.

The other big reason people let possessions overtake them is guilt. "Somebody gave it to me." "It's too good to throw away." Fine. That's what the Salvation Army is for—good stuff you don't need anymore. And you can feel virtuous instead of guilty, a win/win situation.

RATIONALIZING

If someone tries to get you to part with your clutter, you can get very defensive and come up with all kinds of excuses for hanging on to things. Creative people can come up with some pretty clever rationales. Do any of these sound familiar?

- "But I paid good money for that!" (It's costing you even more to store it. Cut your losses and sell it or give it away.)

- "That was a gift from my late aunt Bess." (How will she know if you toss it?)

- "I might need it someday." (What are the odds you'll be able to find it—or remember you have it—when you need it?)

- "It might come back in style." (By that time it'll be moldy, and you'll want to buy new anyway.)

- "It's a collector's piece." (Is there really a market for used Atari games? Will you live long enough to see it become truly valuable?)

- "That magazine has good information in it." (Donate it to the library and visit it there.)

- "It's hardly been used, it's like new." (That should be your clue. Give it away or sell it.)
- "It doesn't belong to us." (Return it to its rightful owner!)
- "I'm saving this for our grandkids." (Will they want it? If it's not worth displaying or using to you, why would it be worth anything to them? If you're still not sure, give it to your kids and let them decide whether to save it for the grandkids.)
- "I'm going to fix that." (Would it be cheaper to buy a new one?)

There are more—but they're still rationalizations, as in "bogus." Remember, you can't take it with you when you go. As Don Henley points out in a song, "There are no luggage racks on hearses."

Think about what your poor family will have to deal with when you die. They'll have to go through everything you weren't willing to go through when you were alive, make decisions, find homes for stuff, have things appraised, sell stuff off, clean stuff out, rent a Dumpster. Their memories of you may be tarnished by the wish that you hadn't been such a slob. I know it's not a happy thought, but it happens.

My friend Charlie just spent three weeks off from work trying to deal with all the wonderful "stuff" his aunt Esther left behind when she died. He ended up throwing in the towel and going back to Minnesota, leaving the house to a salvage company to clean out and a real estate agent to clean up and sell. Her houseful of tchotchkes didn't help him mourn—they just added frustration and hard work and misery to his loss.

EXCUSES

I didn't bite off more than I could chew—it just grew in my mouth.

—*Dr. Robert Ballard*

Okay, you know you should get rid of at least some of the stuff you've got lying around, collecting dust. You know your life would work better if you organized the junk that *is* worth keeping. So why haven't you done it? As usual, the creative mind can come up with many excuses.

- "I don't have time to organize." (Make the time, because in the long run it will save you time and a half.)

- "My life is too hectic to straighten up and put things away." (Do it in small increments, while you're on hold, waiting for a printout, after a project, once a week.)

- "The mess is overwhelming. I just can't deal with it." (Attack it one pile at a time. A little spot of clean or a picture put up on the wall or a trashcan full of old papers can be inspiring.)

- "Organizing is a waste of time." (Tidiness taken to extremes is a waste of time. But then, so is total disorganization. As long as you know what you have and where it is—and can put your hands on it quickly—you're doing fine.)

- "I'm a creative person." (You can still be a nonconformist and maintain some sort of organization. In fact, by creating your own system, you can make a statement.)

- "What mess?" (If you don't see it, but others are constantly complaining, maybe you should slow down for a minute and take a good look around.)

- "I have more important things to do than clean my desk." (Like what? Watching TV isn't a legitimate excuse; being on deadline for a major project is. And clearing your desk can help you clear your mind and help you get ready to attack that big project.)

GETTING RID OF STUFF

We work to become, not to acquire.
                                        —*Elbert Hubbard*

Some of the things we hang on to, I'll tell you, it's amazing. What's more incredible is that some of it survives through disasters, divorce, and move after move. Nothing is quite as unusual, though, as what renowned big wave rider Greg Noll saved for his friend Rick James.

Over two decades ago, James, while shaping a surfboard in Noll's shop, accidentally cut off his thumb. After Noll rushed his buddy to the hospital, he returned to find the bloody thumb. He cast it in clear resin for safekeeping and kept the thumb on display in his surf shop showcase (where stunned shoppers would suddenly notice it beside the sunglasses and stickers) until Rick came in one day and asked his friend not to put his thumb on display anymore. After that, Noll used the thumb as a paperweight in his office, until he eventually closed his shop.

Now, years later, there is some debate about who owns the appendage. It seems that although the thumb originally belonged to James, Noll has had it in his possession longer. This is a true story!

Maybe you don't have a severed thumb among your clutter, but it's likely that you do have all kinds of other *chozzerai,* much of it pretty worthless, really. Maybe it's time to rid yourself of some of it.

Ask yourself, "When should I toss this?" Answer yourself, "If it's tossable, toss it *now!*" A thing has value only if (and when) you use it, it brings you happiness, or it's valuable. If it doesn't fill these functions, it's tossable.

Something is tossable when it's more trouble than it's worth, when there isn't room to move in your home or office, when it is rotted, rusted, busted, or crusted over, if it is dated, faded, duplicated, or dangerous, ripped, chipped, wrinkled, or a burden in any way.

This is not an easy undertaking. It's tough work on both

a physical and an emotional level. But it can be entirely liberating.

According to Don Aslett, a famous clutter buster and author of *Clutter's Last Stand,* there are ideal times to tackle different pockets of clutter—for instance, when you feel . . .

Angry	Deal with stuff that involves smashing and flattening things.
Happy	Work on old, outdated stuff.
Broke	Go through anything that you may be able to sell.
Energetic	Handle piles that involve a lot of sorting, sifting, and putting things away.
Adventurous	Tackle the attic, basement, or garage.

Other good times to tackle clutter include after doing taxes, changing jobs, upon completion of a big project, on reaching a major milestone (retiring, graduation, birthdays), long weekends, holidays, and especially when you are moving.

The very best time is when you are ready, willing, and able to make a change and take control of your life.

● ●

When These Items Have Outlived Their Usefulness

Item	Shelf Life (Approx.)
Rubber bands	2 yrs.
Mascara	3 mo.
Sunscreen	1 yr.
Lipstick	1–2 yr.
Toothbrushes	3–5 mo.
Canned food	1 yr.

Nail polish	1 yr.
Fragrances	2 yrs.
Pens	2 yrs.
Eyeliner	3–5 mo. (or when too short)
Barry Manilow eight tracks	0
Calendars	Get real!

(Check expiration dates on all medications.)

● ●

WHERE TO START

*At some point in life, the world's beauty becomes
enough. You don't need to photograph, paint, or
even remember it. It is enough. No record of it needs
to be kept and you don't need someone to share it
with or tell it to. When that happens—that letting
go—you let go because you can.*

—Toni Morrison (*Tar Baby*)

The tendency for the creative person is to try to do it all at
once. Because you can see the big picture so clearly, you want
it done already. This approach doesn't work, mainly because
you will burn out before you finish, quit, and never go back
to it, saying, "See, I told you I can't get organized, I'm an
artist."

The owner of a card shop I frequent says she gets up an
hour early and tackles an area of her home before she comes
in to work. After doing this for several weeks, she got her
entire home in order, without any stress. On the other hand,
an artist friend of mine complains that her house is too messy
for the housekeeper to make any headway. She spends half a
day putting things away so her "help" can find surfaces to
clean.

Here are some approaches you may want to consider taking when first starting out.

- **Think small.** Be realistic. Do a little at a time. It boosts your confidence when you can step back and see the fruits of your labor.

- **Go for the worst areas first,** while your enthusiasm for organizing is highest. Look for areas where clutter "nests" or the area that bugs you the most.

- **When cleaning out things you don't need,** go for the easy kills first. Bail the obvious junk. Work up slowly to those hard decisions.

- **Dump anything you haven't worn or used in two years.**

- **Don't pull everything out of a closet.** It's too much to tackle at once, and then you're left with an even bigger mess.

- **Don't overlook areas like the top of the fridge,** windowsills, bookcases, your toolbox, CDs, under the bed, under the porch, your jewelry box, rental storage, RV, boat, under the sink, laundry room, studio, under the desk.

- **Get help!** Invite your mate, co-worker, or neatnik friend to help you work through your mess. Before you start working with someone else, however, relax, take a few deep breaths, and promise not to get defensive. They can help. Let them.

If working with someone you know involves too much emotional baggage, hire a professional organizer. It's amazing what they can do with your mess. If you don't know where to find one, contact the National Association of Professional Organizers, 1033 La Posada Dr., Suite 220, Austin, TX 78752.

MORE TIPS

Don't put it down, put it away.

—*Kathy Peel*

Haven't got enough yet? Try these on. And when you're done, make up your own.

- **Don't get sidetracked** by reading old magazines or old letters. Do what you set out to do or you'll never finish.

- **Set a date** for a party at your place and send out the invitations to give you a firm deadline to get cleaned up.

- **Make a subpile of undecideds** and get through a whole pile quickly. Otherwise you'll catch paralysis by analysis. Just don't put everything in the undecided pile. You can make *some* of those decisions.

- **Don't love something that can't love you back.** Dump it.

- **Ask yourself** these questions as you consider a whether to keep or toss something: What's the worst thing that would happen if I got rid of this? Is this a duplicate of something I already have? Is this something I could borrow? Do I need to keep this for legal reasons? Do I use it often? Is it difficult to replace? Does it work? Can I get parts for it? Do I have a place for this? Does it fit me now? Can I buy a new and better one if I need it someday? Is it valuable? Historical? Is it time-consuming to maintain and clean this thing? Is it worth it? Has the expiration date passed? Is it obsolete? If I lost everything in a fire and had to start all over again, would I replace this item?

- **If you aren't sure** about whether to keep or toss, put it in a holding box. Ask someone to hold it for you, or do it yourself, and date the box. If you didn't need it or miss it in a year, bail it.

- **Start a small drawer to hold undecided stuff.** When it's full, weed it out. Do *not* start another "undecided" drawer.

- **Keep some part of a memento** rather than the whole item. Keep old army medals—you can display them— but give away or sell the uniform to a surplus store.

- **Tear out the best recipes** from a cookbook rather than keeping the whole thing. If you are a vegetarian, save only the recipes that don't include meat.

- **Take a picture of it.** If you have tons of trophies, take a picture of them and display the photo.

- **Make art out of your stuff.** I have a friend who loves earrings, but it got to where she could never find the other half of a pair, the right back to one, or the pair that went with her outfit. She finally put up a corkboard in her bedroom and displayed her earring collection. It looks fabulous, it's an interesting addition to the decor, she can always find the earrings she needs, and she doesn't forget what she has.

- **Save whatever enhances your life.** Keep it where you can see it, use it, show it off. As Bette Midler once said, "Cherish forever what makes you unique, 'cuz you're really a yawn if it goes."

- **Change is good.** If things aren't working for you, in your home or at work, move things around until they do. There is nothing like redecorating to inspire you.

WHAT DO I DO WITH THE STUFF I WANT TO KEEP?

Hard work is often the easy work you did not do at the proper time.

—*Bernard Meltzer*

For the organizationally handicapped, there are sensible ways to deal with the stuff you've decided to keep:

- **Find a place for everything** and then put it in its place. If you take a few seconds to put the item where it belongs now, you can avoid hours of having to pick things up—or search for them—later. Good advice.

- **Group like things and store them together.** (All your golf gear is in one place.)

- **Consolidate and compress.** (If you have two half-empty boxes of the same thing, combine them into one box.)

- **Think multipurpose.** (Those all-in-one gadgets are space-savers. A fax/phone/copier/scanner (and espresso maker) is great.

- **Keep things most often used most accessible.** Open and out. (Coffee cups near coffeemaker on a tree.)

- **Put things where you use them.** (Cookbooks in kitchen. Lint remover in closet. Dishes near eating area.)

- **Put things where they make sense.** (First-aid kit goes in the kitchen, where you're most likely to cut or burn yourself.)

- **Look for and utilize hidden spaces.** (Nooks and crannies between the washer and dryer, for instance.)

- **Shelves!** You could put shelves on all your empty walls—they're a godsend when you have a lot of stuff and you want to get it off the floor but still keep it in plain view.

- **Use wall space** in the closet for an extra bar, shelf, or hook.

- **Put things rarely used in hardest-to-reach places.** (Tux in the hard-to-reach corner of the closet. I guess this depends on your social calendar. Hang it in a clear bag so you can see it.)

- **Empty things like suitcases are hidden storage.** (Empty hatbox for scarves.)

- **Cotton balls and Q-tips** can be out on the counter in an acrylic container.

- **Make a mobile cleaning center** or mini–tool kit that is portable so you can take it where it's needed.

- **Label things clearly.** (Boxes in deep storage, binders on shelf.)

- **Remember: the fewest steps** it takes to put something away, the better.

- **Think convenient, simple, visual, functional.**

- **Create a drop zone.** Put a hamper where you drop clothes or take them off. (Put a bin or basket where clutter collects.)
- **Leave some room for growth, new stuff.** Cramming things into a closet with no extra room guarantees a problem later.
- **Get things off the floor,** especially in the basement, flood areas.

OFFICE

Creative types are disorganized in every area of their lives, except their art form.

—*Kirsten Kirkpatrick*

Comfortable, personable, and workable—that's the ideal office. Sit in your chair, look around. Do you have enough room to work? Can you reach things? Small changes in the ergonomics of your work space can save you hundreds of steps each day.

- **Direct sunlight** and adequate lighting are important.
- **Set up near a window** if you need the inspiration, away from the window if you're easily distracted. Turn your desk away from the door to avoid being distracted by passersby. However, don't sit with your back to the door. It can create an uneasy feeling for many people, and they can't relax.
- **Need quiet or like clamor?** Make sure you're able to control the noise level of your work space.
- **Have plenty of room to spread things out.**
- **Set up near outlets,** phone jacks; minimize wiring clutter (for safety as well as aesthetic reasons).
- **Get a comfortable chair.** Sounds silly, but think about how much time you actually spend in your office chair.

- **Demand adequate storage.** Store archives elsewhere.
- **Use a tool caddy** or file cart for easy access. Make it easy to put things away.

HOME

The more organized your home is, the easier it is to clean. Swipe, wipe, and you're done. Scoop and stash.

- **Store like things together.** If you don't have easy access to an item, you might as well throw it out. Keep things you use most often out on counters or on wall pegs.
- **Set aside a place near the door** for things to take with you, things that need repair, returning, or recycling. This can simply be a particular space on a table or bookcase. If something's in that space, it goes out the door with you.
- **Keep a running shopping list** fastened on the refrigerator door with a magnet.
- **Keep a portable fingernail repair kit** (clippers, emery boards, cuticle cream, polish, cotton balls, nail polish remover, and so on). Use it while watching TV or talking on the phone.
- **Make a portable bin for cleaning supplies,** so you easily can take them with you as you clean each room. This saves time and energy, eliminating the necessity of going back and forth.
- **Keep often used items in more than one place in house.**
- **Keep things out in the kitchen,** hang often used pots and pans, spices, utensils. Make it easy to find things, easy to put them away.
- **Add an extra rod in your closets.** Add hooks, organizers, a freestanding dresser. Make a place to hang dry cleaning, belts, and scarves.

- **Keep a mini–vacuum/cleaning station** with supplies near where you often need to make quick, small cleanups. Like the cat box.

- **Stash sports gear in a trash barrel** with wheels.

- **Make a clipping folder or basket** with coupon-cutting or article-cutting supplies (including scissors so you don't fight. "Where'd you put the scissors?" or "You're not using my best scissors!").

- **Never put a larger item on top of a smaller one** (newspaper over reading glasses), says professional organizer Harriet Schechter. A simple, but effective, tip.

- **Organize clothes by color, type, activity,** whatever works.

- **Keep a basket at the bottom of the stairs,** and put things in it that need to go upstairs. When you go, grab the basket for a single, time- and energy-saving trip.

- **Make it easy for kids to put things away.** Use bins to scoop and stash toys.

CAR

Is your car littered with maps (stick 'em in a clear envelope), receipts, papers, wrappers (use the trash bag), mail, empty containers, cups? Are you so messy that you lose things in the car or are embarrassed to give people a ride? Buy or make a holder for registration and related papers. Find a small backseat bin—it makes it easy to bring things into the house or drop off. A small trash bin can also fit neatly into the backseat. An emergency tub in the trunk should hold flashlight, flares, cables, tools, money.

PHOTOS

- **Dump duplicates** or send them to the people in them. Dump out-of-focus or just plain awful ("I look fat!") pictures when you first go through the prints.

- **Keep your photos in albums.** It helps to keep like photos together—"Vacations," "Christmas"—and label them.

- **A loose-leaf photo album is better than spiral bound—** you can move pages around, add more, make room for captions.

- **Make a "best of" album,** and keep it where you will look at it.

- **A shoebox-style holder with labeled dividers is handy** until you get the photos into an album.

- **Use your photos to make a wall collage.**

- **Make a compilation video of your photos,** and lock it so nobody tapes over it. (Label it. You can dump the originals now.)

- **Keep negatives in a safe place,** easy to grab in case of an emergency. Photos are the most devastating thing to lose in a disaster.

• •

Sentimental Journeys

In his book *Not for Packrats Only*, Don Aslett has a few ideas about what to do with sentimental things that people have a real emotional attachment to. He says:

- Frame it and put it on display.
- Make a collage, montage, sculpture, or scrapbook out of it.
- Give it to someone as a gift.
- Recycle it as something useful. A ceramic coffee mug can become a pencil holder.
- Create a "memory room" or a memory lane (in a hallway).
- Take a picture of it.

• •

HOBBIES

I collect trading cards. That's probably more than you wanted to know about me, but it's applicable here. Here are a few things I've learned over the years about collecting memorabilia:

- **Keep it in a safe, dry place.**

- **Make it accessible** to look at.

- **Keep it all in one place** (Beckett book with cards).

- **Pare it down,** simplify. (Only collect baseball and football by one or two different manufacturers. I figured that one out after I discovered that *Charlie's Angels* trading cards are worthless.)

- **Stop when it stops giving you pleasure.** Oddly enough, it can be hard on others when you stop collecting. My best friend's son used to collect enamel pins—cheap, easy to find, and a nice little gift. He won two blue ribbons at the local fair for his collection. When he lost interest, his friends and relatives lost their best gift idea. Too bad.

• •

Hobbies Engaged in as an Artistic Outlet

Sewing and needlepoint	24.8%
Photography and video	11.6%
Painting	9.6%
Pottery/jewelry	8.4%

—THE NATIONAL ENDOWMENT FOR THE ARTS

• •

TOOLS YOU CAN USE

User-friendly, simple (one step too many may keep you from using it), direct access, visual, colorful, and uncomplicated—these are the things you'll want to incorporate into any organizing system you choose to use.

- **Plastic tubs** and containers that are clear, so you can see what's inside.

- **Clear envelopes,** zip-top bags for important papers, and so on. (Keeps them dry and safe and you can see inside them.)

- **Dividers in drawers** so you can see what's inside, even in the dark.

- **Hooks.** (Hang bike, clothes, kitchen utensils, or gardening tools.)

- **Portable bins or bags,** storage units on wheels (so you can take your work outside).

- **Containers.** (Keep stationery supplies in the car.)

- **Buy cool, colorful, fun new products** to keep things in. Organizers that will make you *want* to organize.

- **Shelves** can help you organize every area of your life. You can't have too many.

- **Stepladder.** To reach the highest of those shelves.

- **Use those old Tupperware containers** to store small, useful things like pushpins, paper clips, screws, pencils . . .

CLUTTER CONTROL

The goal of all inanimate objects is to resist man and ultimately defeat him.

—Russell Baker

The best way to control clutter is to stop it from happening in the first place. In other words:

- **When you go from room to room**, pick something up and drop something off in its place. Paula Jhung, a former flight attendant and author of *How to Avoid Housework*, says, "I learned to never walk from room to room empty-handed. I learned not to walk down an aisle without delivering or retrieving a tray, drink, or child."

- **Think** before you buy.

- **Ask for gifts that won't clutter**—scuba lessons, a vacation, massages, edible things, tickets to a game, housecleaning certificate.

- **Have a junk chair** to consolidate mess to one central place.

- **Have a rack** for your remote controls.

- **Keep a box, bin, or basket** for things you want to scoop up and put away quickly.

- **Fifteen minutes a day keeps the clutter at bay.** Do it during the commercial breaks of your favorite TV show.

- **Things that stay are used daily.** Things within reach are used weekly. In the same room but put away are things used monthly. If they're used only once or twice a year, keep them in another room entirely.

- **Hire a cleaning service.** My friend keeps leaving things out for the maid to pick up. Hello, Nicholas, you don't *have* a maid!

- **Always be on the lookout** for ways to do things better.

- **My favorite idea:** Get a larger trashcan.

● ●

One of Us

INTERVIEW WITH HAIRSTYLIST RONA DORFMAN

Tell me about your work space and how it works for you.

Well, the space is very small, number one, so I have to use it in the way that I need it and the way that works best.

If you had more space, how would you use it?

Would I clutter up more of it? Probably. If I had a bigger counter, there would be more stuff on there. During the day, I don't usually tidy up between clients because I don't have time and I don't want to take time to clean up. I just go to the next one because I'm making more money that way. Why take the time to clean up when I can take another customer? I feel it's a waste of time during the day to continually organize and clean.

How do you think others view your organizing style?

They probably say, "My God, she's messy! She's sooo untidy." I mean, I do have someone sweep up the hair and throw the towels in the hamper, but that's about it.

How do you see it?

That I'm working hard. I'm doing something. I'm being constructive. I'm not tidying up all the time, because my chair is never empty, it's always got somebody in it. I'm using my time better and not wasting time cleaning up—hair, that is.

When do you straighten up?

At the end of the day I clean up, wipe everything up, put everything away where it should be. So in the morning when I come in, I can start fresh.

• •

12

• • • • •

WHAT PART OF "NO" DON'T YOU UNDERSTAND?

"No!"—The Greatest Time-Saver of All Time

Saying "no" can be the ultimate self-care.
—*Claudia Black*

Everyone—your mate, children, parents, family members, friends, boss, clients, co-workers, and neighbors—wants a piece of your time. Before you try to meet their requests (or demands), examine your own needs.

LOSING BATTLES
By Natasha Josefowitz, Ph.D.
By trying to be
everywhere at once
I am nowhere

By trying to be
everyone to too many
I am no one

From dusk till dawn, it's go, go, go. You cram as much as you can into each waking minute. No doubt about it, you're a busy individual. Yet how much of what you do is what you *want* to be doing? *Should* be doing? How much do you continue to do because you don't know how to say that you need a break?

The fact is, people will take advantage of you only as long as you let them. It is totally within your power to make better decisions about how you dole out your time. The first thing you need to learn is how to say "no." Repeat after me: "No!" Feels good, doesn't it? This one word can help you gain control of your life again.

Why People Say "Yes" When They Really Mean "No"

That woman can speak eighteen languages, and she can't say "no" in any one of them.

—Dorothy Parker

Answer these questions honestly to find out if you are a "yes" person.

1. You really believe you can do it all, and you're trying to prove it—unsuccessfully.

2. You overestimate how much time you have available.

3. You hate to reject anyone, and you would rather say "yes" than hurt their feelings.

4. You want to be liked, you want to please others (at the expense of your own happiness).

5. You're afraid you'll miss a great opportunity, even though you don't have the time to do your best work.

6. You are just honored to be asked, so you say "yes" without thinking.

7. You don't want to be left out, so you agree to be a part of something you don't have the time for.

8. You believe only you can do the job.

9. It sounds like more fun than what you're supposed to be doing, so you say "yes."

10. You say "yes" to keep busy because you are afraid to face own problems.

11. You want to be seen as a team player.

12. You're afraid you'll lose your job or your client if you ever say "no."

Why Others Take Advantage of You

- You don't value your own time, so why should others?
- Low self-esteem makes you afraid to stand up for yourself.
- You lead people to believe you can and want to take on more.
- You brag about being able to do it all.
- Others value their priorities more than yours, and you let them.
- Others trick you into it or use your guilt against you.
- You're easily bored and all too eager to move on to something new.
- You're impulsive, and say "yes" without thinking.
- People know you can't say "no," so they use you as a dumping ground for things they don't want to do.

WHY NOT SAYING "NO" IS A PROBLEM

The only power an actor has is the ability to say "no."
—*Kathleen Turner*

Saying "no" can cause you some temporary discomfort. There is a lot of social pressure to "be nice," after all. But *not* saying "no" can cause you a lot worse than a twinge of guilt or a momentarily irritated spouse or co-worker. For instance:

- You end up becoming a jack of all trades, master of none. Everything you do ends up being a rush job, and nothing is done particularly well or on time.

- While you are busy helping others with their projects, your own more important projects and commitments suffer.

- Eventually you end up being overcommitted and burned out. You have no time left to be creative as you rush from project to project.

- You end up being seen as a flake because you can't finish things on time. This damages your reputation and can

cause permanent harm to your livelihood. You can ultimately be seen as incompetent—which is ironic, because
many people feel that if they *don't* take on everything
offered to them, they will be seen as incompetent.

- You end up regretting your decisions and resent the
  person you agreed to help out.

- You take on projects and assignments that may be
  unethical, immoral, or illegal because you were afraid to
  say "no." This is a worst-case scenario, but it happens.

Remember, everything you say "yes" to is a "no" to
something else. Think about that for a minute. A "yes" at
work can be a "no" to your family. A "yes" to a friend can
mean "no" to a lucrative offer at work. Most often, however,
you're the one who suffers when you can't say "no" and over-
commit yourself. Keep the following two things in mind:

- **Never make a promise you can't keep.**

- **Never say "yes" without thinking about it first.** Try
  temporizing. Say, "Let me check my calendar, and I'll
  get back to you."

LIFE'S TOO SHORT: WHEN, WHAT, AND WHOM TO SAY "NO" TO

*Time is the only coin you have in life . . . and only
you can determine how it will be spent. Be careful
lest you let other people spend it for you.*
—Carl Sandburg

Time is like money in many ways—only in my opinion it is far
more valuable. How you handle either ultimately affects your
life. It's your choice whether you save or spend your money,
whether you save or spend your time, whether you invest it in
something worthwhile or fritter it away on meaningless things
until there's none left over for what you really want.

Others will try to steal your time, often with no evil intent (just lack of consideration). You can be overly generous and face bankruptcy—physical and emotional—when you simply run out of time. You can't spend what you don't have. You can go to jail for passing off bad checks. What you suffer from giving away your time is, in some ways, far worse.

Are you tired of being pushed around, taken advantage of? The key to winning your life back is a two-letter word—n-o. Be more selective with that other word, yes. Know your limit, when enough is enough. Be first in line for your time. If you are burned out and need to relax (have a "Blockbuster night"), do it. The more you give in to get along or go along, the less you like yourself and the less you like other people.

Know what your priorities are and build your time around those. Say "yes" when you choose to, when it's right for you. Saying "no" to activities you hate doing is a terrific feeling. Saying "no" to things you'd like to do but just don't have the time for isn't as great, but the feeling of having enough time to do the things already on your plate—that makes up for anything.

● ●

Exercise

- List three things you want to do but never have the time for. (It's easier to say "no" when you know what meaningful thing you *could* be doing.)
- List one thing you do but want to stop doing.
- List the most important people in your life. How much time do you give to them? Is it enough? Do you need to improve in this area?
- If I had more time I would . . . (Finish this sentence.)
- List something you continue to do just to please someone else but resent having to do.
- List things you said "yes" to but now wish you had said "no" to.

● ●

IMPORTANT QUESTIONS

Being strong in no way implies being powerful, manipulative, or even forceful. By operating from strength, I mean leading your life from the twin positions of worth and effectiveness.

—Dr. Wayne Dyer

When you start your day, look at your calendar or "to do" list and ask, "What can I drop today?" Cut the fat! Learn to pause before you say "yes." Give yourself at least a moment to ask yourself some questions before you respond. Cover with an "Ahhhhh" or say, "Let me check my calendar."

- Next time you are tempted to say "yes," stop and think, What am I doing? What should I be doing? What should I do next? What should I not do?

- If you say "yes," what will you get for it? What will you have to give up? Is saying "yes" worth the trade-off?

- Ask yourself if the things you are spending the bulk of your time on are bringing you closer to your goals or taking you further away.

- Ask, "Does this fit into my life?"

- Ask, "Why should I do this?"

- Ask, "If I say 'no,' what is the worst thing that will happen?" Can you live with that?

- Ask, "Will it matter a year from now whether I did it or not?"

- Ask, "What will I really be missing out on or losing if I turn this down?"

WHEN NO REALLY MEANS NO
(SAY IT WITHOUT LOSING YOUR JOB
AND YOUR FRIENDS)

People can't walk all over us unless we lie down.
—*Ann Landers*

There are ways to say "no" gently, without alienating people or losing (many) clients and friends. While I was concentrating on this book, I said "no" to everybody. It was even on my answering machine message. "I'm very busy with a project just now, so I might not get back to you until after the fifteenth." Few people had a problem with this (well, my wife did)—they had an explanation and a time limit. But God help me on the fifteenth.

Other ways to help yourself to "no" include

- **Save one day a month for yourself,** to catch up, recharge, plan, think, create. Make it sacred. When people say, "Oh, he's never available on the twelfth," you're doing it right.

- **Block out time on your calendar** for your vacation, projects, prep time. This way, that time is filled when you check your calendar. It's easier to say "no" and back it up by pointing at your full calendar. (Don't let them get close enough to see what it's filled by—that's none of their business.)

- **Even if your calendar is empty,** you don't have to say "yes."

- **Wait a minute.** Think before you speak.

- **Turn down things that have the potential to damage your reputation,** career, integrity, respect of peers. Be polite, but firm. "I'm just not comfortable with that."

- **Say "no" to negative people** who drain your energy, upset you, don't appreciate what you do for them, are takers. Don't give in. Be consistent, and eventually they'll stop asking.

- **Set some guidelines:** no phone after seven P.M., no dinner meetings, no lunch meetings.

- **Don't be afraid to lose clients** who are more trouble than they are worth. Sometimes saying "no" or holding to firm limits brings them into line and they're easier to work with. Sometimes they leave in a huff. It's a chance you take.

- **When you do say "yes,"** make sure that "yes" is valuable. If you don't value your time, others won't, either.

- **If you know you want to say "no," say it quickly.** Dragging it out with a "maybe" gives them false hope and delays the inevitable. Then you have to call back, which takes time, and you open yourself up to cajoling, guilt, and the likelihood that you'll cave in to pressure.

- **Offer a counterproposal,** an option, or another solution that won't take up as much of your time. Refer to others. Offer to help at a later date.

- **Role-play** and practice saying "no" with a friend.

- **The truth will set you free.** In the hit movie *Liar, Liar,* Jim Carrey plays an attorney who is compelled to tell the truth for twenty-four hours, which changes his entire life—for the better. Be honest when it comes to saying "no." You won't have to remember all your little lies or worry about running into someone when you're supposed to be out of town. You won't have to explain your tan to your boss when you said you were home sick.

- **The truth often hurts.** You don't have to hurt someone's feelings in order to say "no" to them. Don't say, "Your kids are little monsters, you can't possibly pay me enough to watch them again." Be more tactful—after all, this poor person has to live with those horrors. Say, "I'm sorry, I just don't seem to get on well with the little . . . er, kids."

- **You don't have to give a reason.** Be firm, polite. Keep explanations short, simple. "I'm booked solid." "I can't, sorry." "I'm afraid you'll have to find somebody else." Keep moving.
- **If you do offer an explanation, don't argue it.** Stick to your guns and get off the phone, turn back to your work, walk away.

DECISIONS

More than any time in history, mankind faces a crossroads. One path leads to despair and utter hopelessness. The other, to total extinction. Let us pray we have the wisdom to choose correctly.

—*Woody Allen*

"Regular or decaf?" That was the question facing the woman in the Honda commercial. She seemed to be overwhelmed by this simple choice. It paralyzed her and rendered her unable to decide. Regular or decaf. It's not the difficulty of the question, but the sheer volume of questions we face every day that bogs us down. They seem to have a cumulative effect.

To make matters worse, in our fast-paced society, people expect you to decide immediately. *Right now.*

Decisions take time. We make hundreds of decisions every day. What to do (and not do), what to do first, when to do it, and the best way to do it. You have a limited amount of time, so your most important decision is how to use your time.

For the creative person, decision making is not generally a strong suit for a number of reasons. As a divergent thinker, you have endless options. This complicates the process. You're also likely to be wishy-washy about choices when everything that looked interesting yesterday seems boring today. Being intuitive and emotional can be beneficial in the decision-making process but can just as easily lead you astray. Trusting your gut without doing any research can lead to problems down the road. Listening to your heart without consulting your head also makes for hasty, impulsive choices that may prove disastrous. These difficulties can complicate all aspects of your life.

That doesn't mean you can't make good choices. By combining your natural right-brain tendencies with solid left-brain techniques, you can make good, solid decisions that stick. This is important because it is your choices that directly affect the condition of your life—all areas of your life.

Some points to ponder when you are making decisions:

- **You can control only your own choices,** not other people or outcomes.

- **There's no such thing as "no decision."** The inability to say "yes" is the same as saying "no." People who fail are those who can't make decisions.

- **Look for win-win decisions.**

- **Realize that you can't have it both ways.** So look for the better of the two choices.

- **Make a sound decision and** *stick with it.*

- **You have the power to choose,** whether you like your options or not. Don't let others make important choices for you.

- **Think long-term.** One of the biggest mistakes you can make when faced with a big decision is to only consider how your choice affects you in the short term. Consider the long-range ramifications of your choice.

HOW TO MAKE GOOD CHOICES

Some rainy winter Sunday when there's a little boredom, you should carry a gun. Not to shoot yourself, but to know exactly that you are always making a choice.

— Lina Wertmuller

The ideal way for a creative person to approach a decision is to combine a left-brain (analytical and logical) approach with a right-brain (intuitive and emotional) approach. Here is an example of the two different but equally valid styles of decision making.

LEFT BRAIN. Give yourself plenty of time to read and research the options available, gather together all the facts, and review them, weigh the odds, talk it over with those involved, seek input from others, make a pro and con list, and come to a logical decision. Then stick by it, regardless of the outcome.

RIGHT BRAIN. You acknowledge a force outside yourself, so you meditate, find a quiet place to think and get inside yourself, get in touch with intuition, and, in a moment of clarity, take a leap of faith. Then, when new possibilities present themselves, change directions and flip-flop your decision.

Neither of these styles is wrong or even better than the other. When you combine the two, you end up with the best choice.

Here are some additional techniques to help you when facing an important decision:

- **Don't waste much time on trivial decisions,** like which brand of pens you should buy, looking for that perfect card, or choosing just the right font for that letter to your pen pal. Ask yourself, "How important is this decision and how much time does it deserve?"

- **Set a deadline for collecting data or options.** You can never get it all. If you try to wait for the time when you have exhausted all research, you end up with a more difficult problem—paralysis by analysis.

- **Narrow down your options** by eliminating the obvious weak ones. If you are considering a move, for instance, narrow it down by determining what's important. If climate is important (you want to live in a warm one), you can eliminate Fargo, North Dakota, without a whole lot of thought. (Oh, jeez.)

- **Keep an eye on the long-term effects** and think about how this affects those around you.

- **Allow yourself time to ponder** before you make a big decision. Time to think before you act helps you avoid conflicts, potential problems, and unnecessary work. Very few things require a snap decision, so think it through. In "Scandal in Bohemia" Sherlock Holmes said, "It is a capital offense to theorize before one has data."

- **Don't drag it out too long** in hopes that it will go away. Eventually you will have to deal with it. The longer you stall, the harder it gets—and sometimes the more it costs you. Even if there might be something better out there, is it worth the wait?

- **Don't let the fear of a poor choice keep you from making a choice at all.** First of all, there is no such thing as a perfect choice. Most choices leave you with a little anxiety and remorse. If you truly do make a poor choice, though, take heart—most decisions are reversible. If the worst happens and you can't undo it, learn from it and move on. As Harry S Truman said, "Whenever I make a bum decision, I just go out and make another."

- **Check your response.** Sigmund Freud recommended that when all choices are equal, flip a coin. Then note what the coin indicates. Look into your reaction. Are you pleased? Disappointed? This should help you to come to the right decision. When I finished college, my dad offered me a position in his company. The other choice was to start my own company. It was too close to call, so I flipped a coin. It came up that I should work for my dad—so I flipped again! Decision made.

EXERCISE

Make two decisions you have been putting off, an easy one and a more difficult one you have been postponing. Do it now.

Epilogue

·····

NO GOALS, NO GLORY

Don't Be Afraid of the "G" Word

The man who starts out going nowhere, generally gets there.

—Dale Carnegie

Wait! Wait! Don't skip this chapter. I know the mere mention of the word "goals" might make your eyes heavy and bring on a giant yawn. "Goals? Oh yeah, didn't I see some late night infomercial on TV by some guy hawking audiotapes about goals the other night?" you will say. You see goals as boring, constricting, and unnecessary. (By the way, the fact that you were up at that ungodly hour watching an infomercial is a sure sign you should read this chapter.)

This is important and exciting stuff. It's about making your dreams come true. It's about a better and more fulfilling life. It's about coming to a clearer understanding of who you are, what you want, and how to get it.

I know many creative people who mistakenly believe that they don't need to set goals, even after I tell them that the many celebrities and business leaders I have interviewed and befriended all sing the praises of having some form of a goal.

You don't have to focus solely on the future; you certainly shouldn't forsake enjoying the present. And your goals don't have to be huge. Simply get to know yourself, who you are, what you enjoy doing and do well, and put your whole heart into doing the best you can, today, tomorrow, and next week. Choose a path and stick with it, all while enjoying the pursuit.

It's that simple. Really.

You may think you already have goals. Are they written down? If your goals are only in your head, they're not goals. They're *wishes*. Occasionally wishes come true, but not nearly as often as goals do.

In the movie *Back to the Future III*, "Doc" Brown says to Marty (Michael J. Fox's character), "Your future is whatever you make it—so make it a good one." That's what this chapter is about. Goal setting is a creative form of time travel, a way of reaching into the future, *your* future.

You'll be surprised at how fun, flexible, and easy this process can be. Tap into your ability to daydream and see the big picture—use the power of your intuition and imagination to creatively design a future and map out a way to get there. (I promise this will be worth your while and not boring.)

YOU NEED GOALS IF YOU FEEL . . .

- Your life or your work is spinning out of control.
- You don't have enough time, money, or energy.
- Your career is not where you want it to be.
- You feel lost and confused, don't know what to do next.
- You're unhappy, unmotivated, and unsatisfied at home or at work.
- You want it all and are overwhelmed by choices.
- Your life lacks passion and purpose.
- You feel regret or guilt not for the things you did, but for those you didn't do.
- You don't know what you want.

A MILLION SUCCESSFUL PEOPLE CAN'T BE WRONG

Positive changes can't happen without goals.
— *Tony Robbins*

You don't have to be totally miserable or unsuccessful for goals to help you. I have a friend who was quite successful, with an interesting, busy business, a happy marriage, and a great kid. She didn't make as much money as she wanted to and had little time for traveling or relaxing with friends and family. But she thought she was doing all right. Whenever things started to fall apart, a new opportunity came her way, sending her off in yet another direction. She felt this broadened her horizons, and life was certainly never dull.

I talked to her about setting goals, and she said, "Lee, I'm forty years old and I still don't know what I want to be when I grow up. Maybe what I want is *not* to grow up, but I'm not going to write *that* down for anybody else to see."

An intelligent, creative person, she could see that the possibilities for her were nearly endless, and she hated to limit herself by choosing one. I helped her focus on a single goal, a financial one. She wrote it down and stuck it in her desk, where she saw it every time she opened her drawer for a pen and was reminded every time she wrote up a bid on a new job. Within two years she had reached that goal and was ready to use the technique to get in control of other aspects of her life—like time.

You need to start *somewhere*. If you're not ready to put your whole life in focus, find a part of it that you can work on.

My first goal, back when I was cutting class to hang out at the beach, as a teenager was to make honor roll by the next semester. I wrote the goal on a piece of paper and put it in my wallet (which was otherwise empty). Woody Allen once said that 80 percent of success was just showing up. I took his words to heart, went to class, applied myself, and—lo and behold! I made honor roll. My parents thought it was a miracle.

Since reaching that first goal, I set and reached my goals

of opening a retail store (which became a chain) and a publishing company (which I still own), becoming an author (six books to date), starting an Internet-based business, traveling the country as a trainer, getting married before age thirty (I cut it close—twenty-nine) . . . The list goes on.

My parents no longer believe in miracles. They believe in goals.

Don't be afraid that goals will rule your life—rather, they let *you* rule your life. And don't be afraid to admit what you want and go after it.

POWs and concentration camp survivors have said the reason for their survival was a sense of future vision, a sense of meaning, a conviction that they still had important work left to do. Future-oriented thinking and a sense of mission kept them alive. With this simple tool, you can handle challenges you thought impossible, overcome fears, doubts, insecurities, and fatigue.

Goal setting is a powerful process that allows you to focus your energy, creativity, and time. Having a firm handle on what you want helps you focus on doing the right things. Just doing the exercises in this chapter can help you unleash your creative powers.

SPINNING YOUR WHEELS

There are many things in life that will catch your eye, but only a few will catch your heart. Pursue those.

—Unknown

A few years ago, a friend of mine decided to go for his fixed-wing pilot's license, and he talked me into getting mine as well. From the very beginning, however, it felt wrong. It was expensive and time-consuming, and although I enjoyed my time in the air, I didn't like all the time spent studying. Then I read a story in *Pilot* magazine about a pilot who crashed and died despite over two thousand hours of flying time, and it hit me. My larger goal in life is to live— a long time.

After nine hours of flying, I quit. It felt great. Flying was not something I really wanted—it was what my friend wanted, and I resented it. (Ironically, he talked me into it while we went parachuting together, another hobby I have since dropped.)

Nobody can tell you what you want or even what you *should* want. To set viable goals, you've got to think for yourself and be honest—whether you want to be a belly dancer or an astronaut, a sculptor or a mommy, or all of the above and more.

BRINGING YOUR DREAM INTO FOCUS

If you can dream it, you can do it. Always remember that this whole thing was started by a mouse.

—Walt Disney

Setting goals is actually a voyage of self-discovery, and as such, many people shy away from it. I'll make it easy for you. Just answer the following questions. Don't think too much, don't spend a lot of time, take it in any order. Be honest, and don't let anybody look over your shoulder. Have fun.

Write your responses down, draw them, or cut out pictures to illustrate them. Just get an answer to each question onto paper in some form that you can understand later.

Put the pages away for a couple of days and then come back to them. Reread your answers and see what you think after letting the questions percolate in your subconscious for a while. Then make any changes, additions, or fine-tuning you need.

There. You have the basis for a written set of goals. It isn't so hard—but it will be quite illuminating (and much cheaper than psychoanalysis).

THE BIG PICTURE

Everyone has an opinion of what "success" really means. This is especially true for the creative person. In order to achieve success, you must define it, in your own words.

A friend of mine, Lambert Davis, a talented illustrator of children's books, admitted one day, "When I first started doing children's books, I did some serious soul-searching, wondering if this was below other forms of illustrating. What would my art school cronies think? After I actually met some of the kids who were affected by these books, and these kids were stoked, that's when I came to the realization this was something I could do for the rest of my life."

1. If you had only six months to live, what would you do?

2. What would you like your tombstone to say?

3. If you could do anything, what would you do?

4. If you knew nobody was looking, what would you try?

5. Is there anything/anybody you would secretly love to be?

CAREER/BUSINESS

Tom Clancy was an obscure defense analyst for years. Not a bad career, but not his passion, his dream. His true calling was to be a writer. After he followed his dream, he became one of the most successful novelists in the world. In interviews Clancy has said he is happier and, certainly, wealthier. To wake up knowing you are doing exactly what you are supposed to be doing, something you truly enjoy, is the number one key to success and happiness.

6. As a kid, what did you want to be when you grew up?

7. If you could change careers with anyone, who would it be? Why?

8. If money were no object, what career would you choose?

9. If you knew you could not fail, what type of business would you start?

10. How would you describe success?

FUN AND ADVENTURE

Burnout is a real problem for creative people. It can leave you sick, it can make you procrastinate or do stupid things just because you don't want to do what you're supposed to do, it can stop you cold in the middle of a project with nowhere to go. You can forestall burnout by giving yourself a break, taking trips, playing, laughing, living your life to the fullest. Step away from work now and then, and give yourself a chance to remember that there really are no barriers between work and play, between imagination and reality, between giving and taking. This is your strength as a creative person.

11. What's the one thing you have most fun doing?

12. Name one place you have always wanted to go.

13. If you could lighten up, what silly thing would you do?

14. Name something you're tempted to try, even though it sounds crazy.

15. Name something you used to enjoy but don't do much anymore.

FAMILY/FRIENDS

Pete, a former friend of mine, taught me a valuable lesson about family and friends. Pete was always trying to hit a home run, make the big score. At first we thought it was funny. We would say, "Oh, that Pete, it's always something new."

Then he discovered multilevel marketing, and it wasn't funny anymore. He was so gung ho it was all he talked about. It got to the point where I wouldn't take his calls, because I knew he was trying to sell me. I never bought into his "deal of a lifetime." His parents and brother did, though. They lost over $25,000, and Pete lost both his money and his wife. He kept telling her, "When this takes off, then we can spend some time together," until she finally left him. Today, Pete is bankrupt both literally and emotionally.

16. What are the three most important relationships in your life?

17. Describe those relationships—how they are, how you want them to be.

18. How much time do you spend with each of these people every week?

19. What could you do today to improve or enhance each one?

20. Anyone you wish you could make up with?

21. Feel guilty about anyone, anything? Why?

22. Are you there when your friends and family need you? Do you feel you know when that is?

PERSONAL/FITNESS

Despite being overweight, Richard Simmons was a successful actor and model (he appeared as a grape in one of the early Fruit of the Loom commercials) before he was "Sweatin' to the Oldies" Richard Simmons. He was successful but didn't feel good about himself. One day he found a note on his car that read "Fat people die young. Please don't die.—An Admirer."

Simmons immediately went on a crash diet, lost over a hundred pounds in three months—and landed in the hospital. After this devastating experience, he learned how to lose weight safely through proper exercise and good nutrition. Today he's half the man he used to be, and I mean that in a good way. He has helped many others battle the bulge.

23. Name the three things you want people to think of when they hear your name.

24. If you could live your life over, what would you change?

25. What is the one thing you feel your life is missing?

26. Name five tiny changes you would like to make in yourself/your life.

27. Finish this sentence: "I wish I had . . ."

28. List three classes you could take, three skills you wish you had.

29. Name one thing you'd like to do but never get around to.

30. If you could do one thing better, what would it be?

31. What is your ideal weight/size?

CREATIVE

As a stand-up comic, Gary Shandling entertains audiences by poking fun at himself and his inadequacies. He would have us believe he is insecure, wishy-washy, and overwhelmed by life. Nothing could be further from the truth. He is a confident and creative individual who sets goals, focuses on them until they are achieved, and then boldly moves on to new, more challenging ones.

Before he was a success in front of the camera, Shandling made a name for himself behind the scenes as one of Hollywood's top situation comedy writers. He was at the top of his game and making an excellent living when, in 1977, a freak auto accident nearly took his life. (He was in a fender-bender, and when he got out to inspect the damage, a third car rammed into the scene and crushed him between the first two vehicles.) He was hospitalized in critical condition, and his full recovery took weeks. While healing, he had a chance to reflect on his life. He decided he should break free of his frustrating yet lucrative career as a television writer and take on the riskier but more creative career of stand-up comic.

32. Name one way you could improve your life by using your creativity. Your job?

33. How much time do you spend watching TV? On creative pursuits?

34. What creative project have you started but never followed through on?

.35. What projects do you want to do but never seem to find the time for?

36. What do you consider your real creative strength?

I am not against having personal possessions if they bring you joy, security, or peace. At the marina where I hang out, there are people who are obsessed with having the biggest, best boat, and they spend all their time working to afford it and then working to maintain it. They have no time to enjoy the camaraderie, friendships, family trips, solitude, or clean, open atmosphere of the ocean and bay.

Things won't bring you lasting happiness. Having too many things, or making possessions too important a part of your life, can actually cause stress.

According to a survey by the Merck Family Fund, 28 percent of working adults say they voluntarily reduced their income in the past five years because of changing priorities. Money is no longer a true measure of success.

37. If you could possess any one thing, what would it be?

38. If money were no object, what would you do?

39. List ten items you would like to own but don't.

40. Write your own obituary (from the movie *Cocktail*, by Brian Flanigan).

41. How much money do you need each year to be financially secure?

FLASH FORWARD

The only limit to what you can achieve is the extent to which you can clearly define it.

—*Anonymous*

Okay, take a good look at your answers to the foregoing questions. They should help you put together a list of "I wants," at least one for each of the following categories:

- Personal (self-improvement, health, recreational)
- Relationships (spiritual, family, friends)

- Career (professional accomplishments)
- Financial (possessions, wealth)

Write out your "I want" list as simply and clearly as you can. These are your "goals." It's that easy. Don't feel limited by the categories I chose; they're there just to help you see how many areas your written goals should cover. Refine a bit, and you're on your way.

SIMPLIFY

Just get it down on paper, and then we'll see what to do with it.

—*Maxwell Perkins*

I realize that this is as far as you may want to take this process. That's fine. So I'll provide you with some simple solutions to help you work on the goals you've identified. Keep in mind that the two most important steps are figuring out exactly what you want and stating it clearly.

Put your goals in a form that you can refer to every day. They're your guidance system, your steering, so they must be in some form your brain can use. There's no one way that's right for everyone. Here are some methods that have worked for other creatives. Choose whatever works for you or invent your own.

- Find an object that represents the main goal you are trying to accomplish and keep it on your desk. It could be a toy or sculpture, as long as it symbolizes to you the direction you are heading in or something you want.

- I use a dream board to illustrate what I want. I cut up dozens of magazines to get pictures representing my goals and ways I would reward myself for reaching my goals. I pasted them on a foam-core board and keep it in my office where I see it every day. Add captions and descriptions under each picture if you like, make it a collage, add your own drawings or different materials. Make it a work of art—like your life.

- Make a master list of your goals and carry it with you or post it where you will see it regularly. You can divide the list by how long it will take you to reach a goal. Or jot down your main goals on an index card and carry it in your purse or wallet, taking it out to look at it whenever you find yourself with a little extra time on your hands.

- You may just want to choose a general direction to head in. Try to get this down in writing, even if it is just a theme for the year. If you can't find the words, use your artistic talents to draw or paint your goal, or use the computer to design a document that illustrates it.

- Put your goals on Post-it notes and paste them on your bathroom mirror, in your car, on the fridge, in the office—anywhere you will see and be reminded of them every day.

- Make a tape recording of your goals and play it back before you go to bed, while driving in your car, or when you're working out. Put them to music, like the theme to *Rocky* or *Chariots of Fire,* whatever motivates you.

- Put your goals on a time line so you can see exactly how long it should take you to get from here to there.

- Make your goals into a board game, moving your player forward every time you achieve a goal.

- Put your goals in a journal or diary. Write a month ahead, as if you had already reached a short-term goal, then read before bed.

- Exchange your goals with a goal buddy. A goal buddy can help keep you on track, motivated, and accountable. Find someone who is positive and encouraging, someone you respect. Exchange goals and meet regularly to share progress reports. An extra benefit is that your buddy will now be on the lookout for people and resources that can help you reach your goals.

- Make your goals into a poem or a song that you sing every day in the shower or recite on the way to work.

- Use a software program to organize your goals by week, month, year. Update your progress the first thing after you turn on your computer in the morning.

- Use a points and rewards system, giving yourself positive reinforcement for every goal you reach.

- Make a goal jar, putting a dollar (or whatever amount you decide) in the jar for every time you watch TV, miss working out, or do something counter to your goal.

- Keep a victory log or a journal to track your progress. Make note of some of your small accomplishments along the way to the big score. It'll do wonders for your self-esteem.

FINAL EXERCISE

For this exercise, all you need is a piece of paper, a pen or pencil, and a trashcan. Now, do each step in the order listed, and don't read ahead.

1. Take a piece of paper and fold it into fours.

2. Tear the paper into four individual pieces.

3. On each piece, write one of your four most treasured dreams.

4. Decide which dream is the most important, can't-live-without dream and assign it number one. Number the remaining goals in order of importance.

5. Take the piece of paper marked goal number four, crumple it, and throw it away.

6. Now do the same for goals two and three. Crumple them up and throw them away.

7. You are now left with your number one most important goal. Take a good look at this goal, then crumple it up and throw it away.

How did that feel? Pretty crappy, I hope. If you don't make the time to pursue your goals, it's like throwing them away. Even if it's only ten minutes a day to work on your invention, manuscript, instrument, health—those ten-minute increments add up. Don't throw your goals away (and all the work we've done up to this point) by not making them a part of your day, every day.

Bibliography

· · · · ·

I applaud the authors who have written these groundbreaking and life-changing books and thank you with all my heart. I apologize that you are all stuck here in the back of the book. You deserve better. (If it's any consolation, you are ahead of the index.)

Ash, Mel. *Shaving the Inside of Your Skull*. New York: Putnam Books, 1996. A quirky look at the underbelly of creative thinking. Very good!

Aslett, Don. *How to Have a 48-Hour Day*. Cincinnati, Ohio: Writer's Digest Books, 1996.

———. *Not for Packrats Only*. Cincinnati, Ohio: Writer's Digest, 1991.

Ayan, Jordan. *10 Ways to Free Your Creative Spirit and Find Your Great Ideas*. New York: Crown Trade Paperbacks, 1997.

Bliss, Edwin C. *Doing It Now*. New York: Simon & Schuster, 1986.

Booher, Dianna. *Get a Life Without Sacrificing Your Career*. New York: McGraw-Hill, 1997.

Burnham, Sophy. *For Writers Only*. New York: Ballantine Books, 1994. The title is misleading. This is a book for everyone from carpenters to cubists.

Buzan, Tony. *Use Both Sides of Your Brain*. New York: Dutton, 1983.

Cameron, Julia, and Mark Bryan. *The Artist's Way*. New York: Putnam, 1992. A must-read for every creative person. (Do your morning pages!)

Caroselli, Marlene, Ed.D. *The Innovative Secretary*. Mission, Kan.: SkillPath Publications, 1996.

Cooper, Ann McGee. *You Don't Have to Go Home from Work Exhausted!* New York: Bantam, 1992.

Cooper, Ann McGee, and Duane Trammell. *Time Management for Unmanageable People.* New York: Bantam Books, 1994. A fun and functional book. I highly recommend it.

Covey, Stephen. *First Things First.* New York: Simon & Schuster, 1994.

Culp, Stephanie. *Streamlining Your Life.* Cincinnati, Ohio: Writer's Digest Books, 1991.

Cutter, Rebecca. *When Opposites Attract.* New York: Penguin, 1994.

Davidson, Jeff. *The Complete Idiot's Guide to Managing Your Time.* New York: Alpha Books, 1995.

Edwards, Betty. *Drawing on the Right Side of the Brain.* Los Angeles: J. P. Tarcher, Inc., 1979.

Eisenberg, Ronni, and Kate Kelly. *Organize Your Office.* New York: Hyperion, 1994.

———. *The Overwhelmed Person's Guide to Time Management.* New York: Penguin Books, 1997.

Felton, Sandra. *The Messies Manual.* Grand Rapids, Mich.: Fleming H. Revell, 1981. Written by the founder, president, and chief messy of Messy's Anonymous.

Godek, Gregory. *1,001 Ways to be Romantic.* Weymouth, Mass.: Casablanca Press, 1993.

Griffith, Joe. *Speaker's Library of Business Stories, Anecdotes and Humor.* Englewood Cliffs, N.J.: Prentice-Hall, 1990.

Grout, Pam. *New & Improved!* Mission, Kan.: SkillPath Publications, 1994.

———. *Treasure Hunt.* Mission, Kan.: SkillPath Publications, 1995.

Hedrick, Lucy H. *Five Days to an Organized Life.* New York: Dell, 1990.

Hemphill, Barbara. *Taming the Paper Tiger*. Washington, D.C.: Hemphill & Assoc., 1989. If you have paper problems (and who doesn't?), this is the book.

Higgins, James M. *101 Creative Problem-Solving Techniques*. Winter Park, Fla.: The New Management, 1994.

Jeffers, Susan, Ph.D. *Feel the Fear and Do It Anyway*. New York: Simon & Schuster, 1994.

Jhung, Paula. *How to Avoid Housework*. New York: Fireside, 1995.

Josefowitz, Natasha, Ph.D. *Managing Our Frantic Lives*. Boulder, Colo.: Blue Mountain Press, 1994.

Kawasaki, Guy. *Selling the Dream*. New York: HarperCollins, 1991. I love this "Guy." A true creative spirit, and one fine writer.

Kelly, Kate, and Peggy Ramundo. *You Mean I'm Not Lazy, Stupid or Crazy!* New York: Simon & Schuster, 1995.

Leboeuf, Michael, Ph.D. *Working Smarter*. New York: Warner Books, 1988.

Lehmkuhl, Dorothy, and Dolores Cotter Lamping, C.S.W. *Organizing for the Creative Person*. New York: Crown Trade Paperbacks, 1993. For organizing your home and office, this is the book for you.

Lockwood, Georgene. *The Complete Idiot's Guide to Organizing Your Life*. New York: Alpha Books, 1996.

Maisel, Eric. *Affirmations for Artists*. New York: Putnam Books, 1996. Small in size, this little book is packed with more words of wisdom than books ten times its size. It belongs on your bookshelf (or on your nightstand).

Mayer, Jeffrey J. *Time Management for Dummies*. Foster City, Calif.: IDG Books, 1995.

McGraw, Nancy. *Organized for Success!* Mission, Kan.: SkillPath Publications, 1995.

Orsborn, Carol. *Solved by Sunset*. New York: Crown Trade Paperbacks, 1995.

Peters, Tom. *The Pursuit of WOW!* New York: Vintage Books, 1994.

Petras, Ross and Kathryn. *The 776 Nastiest Things Ever Said.* New York: HarperPerennial, 1995.

Pollar, Odette. *365 Ways to Simplify Your Work Life.* Chicago: Dearborn Publishing, 1996.

Popcorn, Faith, and Lys Marigold. *Clicking.* New York: HarperCollins, 1996.

Robbins, Anthony. *Giant Steps.* New York: Fireside, 1994.

Roger, John, and Peter Williams. *Focus on the Positive.* Los Angeles: Prelude Press, 1991.

SARK. *Inspiration Sandwich.* Berkeley, Calif.: Celestial Arts, 1995.

Schechter, Harriet, and Vicki T. Gibbs. *More Time for Sex.* New York: Dutton, 1995.

Schlenger, Sunny, and Roberta Roesch. *How to be Organized in Spite of Yourself.* New York: Signet, 1989. If you wonder why you do things the way you do, the answer is in this book.

Scott, Dru. *How to Put More Time in Your Life.* New York: Dutton, 1984.

Shook, Robert L., and Eric Yaverbaum. *I'll Get Back to You.* New York: McGraw-Hill, 1996.

St. James, Elaine. *Living the Simple Life.* New York: Hyperion, 1996.

Thompson, Charles. *What a Great Idea!* New York: HarperPerennial, 1992.

Van Ekeren, Glenn. *Speaker's Sourcebook II.* Englewood Cliffs, N.J.: Prentice-Hall, 1994.

Wild, Russ. *Business Briefs.* Princeton, N.J.: Peterson's/Pacesetter Books, 1996.

Winston, Stephanie. *Best Organizing Tips.* New York: Fireside, 1996. These timesaving and organizing tips are the best from the best.

————. *Getting Organized*. New York: Warner Books, 1978.

Wonder, Jacquelyn, and Priscilla Donovan. *Whole-Brain Thinking*. New York: William Morrow and Company, 1984.

Wycoff, Joyce. *Mindmapping*. New York: Berkley Books, 1991.

Zdenek, Marilee. *Right-Brain Experience*. Santa Barbara, Calif.: Two Roads Publishing, 1983.

We would love to hear from you. Let us know which tools or techniques you found the most helpful. If you have any other time management tips you think could help your fellow creative person, we will do our best to include them along with other updates in our "CreativeLee Speaking" newsletter and Web site.

Contact us at
CreativeLee Speaking™
P.O. Box 4100-186
Del Mar, CA 92014

E-mail: leesilber@earthlink.net

Visit our Web site at: http://www.creativelee.com

(For a free newsletter please send a SASE.)

Index

About the Author

· · · · ·

Lee Silber is a true creative spirit. In addition to being a writer, designer, and musician, he is also the founder of several companies, including CreativeLee Speaking.™ When not traveling the country conducting workshops for the creative person, Lee resides with his wife in Del Mar, California.